The Chaos of COVID

True Stories of Surviving, and Sometimes Thriving, During the Pandemic

By CHI Authors
(Crystal Heart Imprints)

Kelly Nicholson, Lynne Fireheart, J. Lieswald, Tiffany McBride, Regina DuRocher Keefe, Ruth A. Souther, T.L. Woodliff, Sonja Glad, Michelle Angone, Laura Greene, Pam Daniel, Sharron Magyar, Gloria Ferguson, Jean Ferratier, Justina Schacht, Shelley Crouch,

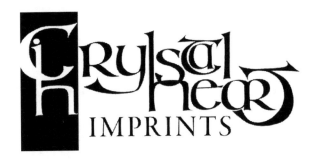

"Human consciousness grows out of nature and the
mind opens in meditation." (Daniel Popper)

DEDICATION

To all CHI authors who bravely speak
their truth through the written word.

ACKNOWLEDGEMENTS

Pam Daniel for her photographic skills and finding the perfect shot for the cover, as well as designing the cover. Terri Woodliff for editing and support of our authors. Ruth Souther for formatting and preparing manuscript for publication.

CONTENTS

Introduction

The pandemic gave us all a giant wallop to the side of the head. It left this nation, and in fact, the entire world, reeling with no sense of when we would become stable. This book is devoted to the stories of all those who went from disbelief and fear to anger and loss, and also to those introverts who practically danced at the idea of a lockdown and the orders to "shelter in place".

You'll find humor, as well as despair. There are sweet tales, as well as ones that are truly heartbreaking, plus stories about fanatical behaviors and those who were out of touch with the reality of our collective situation. We've gathered 16 authors who bravely shared the truth of where they were and what they experienced, on many levels.

We have other authors who, once they began writing, felt the rawness of their own situation and could not finish what they'd started for this book. We have authors who wanted badly to share but were suffering from long COVID and simply didn't have the energy to call forth their painful experiences and write about them.

Crystal Heart Imprints (now known as CHI, as we have evolved our footprint in the bigger world) came into existence in 2009. A handful of us gathered with the desire to have a different sort of writing group, one that was supportive with positive, yet honest, feedback. At that time, we were known as Writing Rituals, and we expanded to also offer publishing support for the authors who were ready.

Currently, we have 25 titles with new projects coming in every year. All of us on the Board are authors with published books—we know what it takes to write, edit, format, and produce the final project.

Our motto is "Everyone has a story." And we set out to prove that truth.

This is not our first CHI collaboration, as we published a collection of stories, poetry, and writing exercises in June 2020: *Writing is Our Super Power* (available on Amazon). We gathered together a year's worth of Writing Ritual workshop material, asked for extra work from those who wanted, and came up with this fun project.

And then we swore we would never do it again. And yet, here we are. These COVID tales are just too important historically to let them fade in our memories. We pray we will never have to live through such a thing again but wanted to preserve the experiences from the 16 authors involved.

If you are interested in CHI, please contact us, we would love to hear from you!

CHI Board: Ruth Souther, Terri Woodliff, Pam Daniel, Sharron Magyar, Nancy Long, Justina Schacht

https://www.crystalheartimprints.com

https://www.facebook.com/Crystalheartimprints

Everyone has a story to tell.

Here are their stories....

Chapter 1

Gasping:
The Experience and Unfiltered Thoughts of a COVID Hospitalization

By Kelly Nicholson

I woke up, gasping for breath and in a panic.

No matter how hard I tried to get air into my lungs, I felt like nothing was getting into my body. My desire for air only led to a coughing fit that left my entire body aching.

I wanted to call out for my mom, but then I remembered—I had moved out three months before. There was no one to hear my pleas to be taken to Union Hospital in Terre Haute, Indiana. My phone was on the other side of my bedroom, and my coughing fit left me so exhausted that the only option was to go back to sleep.

Coughing fits kept waking me up until I couldn't take it anymore. Pushing through the exhaustion that seemed to have settled in my bones, I pulled myself out of the bed, grabbed my phone, and shuffled my way to my chair in the living room on the other side of the house.

I knew that I needed to go to the emergency room but moving from my bed to my chair left me so exhausted that I fell asleep again. It wasn't until I woke up a couple of hours later that I tried to call Mom to get a ride to the hospital. She didn't answer. I had a fleeting thought of calling Dad, but I fell back to sleep.

I can't remember if I eventually called Mom again or if she called me back, but we managed to connect for me to tell her that I needed help.

There is a lot that I have forgotten due to COVID-brain, but I will always remember the looks of terror on my parents' faces when they saw me with my head thrown back against my chair and my mouth wide open like a fish out of water on that Monday morning of April 12, 2021.

Later, when I was in the hospital and couldn't have outside visitors, Mom let it slip during one of our phone calls that Dad broke down over the phone as he updated his oldest brother on my condition. Paired with the memory of my parents' expressions when they first saw me, I felt like I won Worst-Daughter-of-the-Year award.

After getting over the shock, Mom started to gently push me along to get going. She got me some breakfast, helped me get dressed, and loaded me into the car to take me to Union. I did try to wear a mask in the car for Mom's sake, but she quickly told me to take it off. My labored breathing combined with the radio to make the soundtrack of our drive.

All I could think of on the way to Union was getting oxygen. It quickly became an obsession for me because I was certain that I would have such sweet relief once I was given help to breathe.

In my imagination, I thought that when I told the ER

receptionist that I had COVID, she would either have me wait in a different area or offer me an oxygen tank while I waited. I wasn't given a tank and was told to wait in the same area as every other unsuspecting person who needed help. I was bothered that any of those people could contract COVID from me, especially when a mom walked in with her baby.

Thirty minutes had passed, and I was pissed. I was gasping for breath through my mask, and all I could think was, *Where is the fucking oxygen?*

I was ready to either walk up the receptionist desk to yell at her about having a COVID-positive patient wait in the same room as everyone else or push my way to the ER to hook myself up an oxygen tank.

Before I was given the chance to make a fool of myself, I was called back, but I wasn't given help with breathing. As the process to get me admitted into the ER was starting, I kept looking around me for a way to get air into my lungs because I was ready to stick my nose to any nozzle I could find.

While I was looking around, several people kept coming into that screening room. First, a woman came in to get my insurance card and co-payment for visiting the ER. Then, a nurse came in with this cart to do a chest x-ray, and she ended up telling me that I needed to take my glittery shirt and rigidly structured bra off for the test to work because both would have interfered with the machine.

Therefore, two strangers were scarred for life when I was temporarily topless when the payment lady came back with my credit card at the wrong moment.

I don't know why, but previously as I'd walked into EZ Care Clinic in Paris, Illinois, my body broke out in a sweat.

I had sweat dripping down my face as if I had ran a marathon in the middle of summer instead of walking into a medical facility in spring. It was like the virus knew I was about to receive medical attention, and it started to panic.

The staff at EZ Care was very concerned with my sweating, and they kept trying to make me feel comfortable. They kept offering wet paper towels and gave me a shot in the butt for the fever, which I only remembered by reading old texts.

The sweating came back when I arrived at the ER that Monday. The movement of having to take my clothes off and on for the chest x-ray didn't help either.

When Union's ER doctor finally saw me, he took one look at me, and promptly said, "You're the sweatiest COVID patient I have ever seen."

The memory of that moment makes me send a withering glare to anything or anyone who happens to be in my line of sight, but all I could manage at the time was to think, *Excuse me?*

After waiting, stripping, and being insulted, I was finally shown an ER bed where I was given an oxygen tube. I had my first easy breath in hours, and I felt a wave of relief. *I am going to be okay.*

While I had found oxygen, I was attached to the wall to get it. Whenever I needed to go to the bathroom, I had to take the tube off to walk down the hall. During those short trips, I missed my tube.

In hindsight, my idea of busting down doors to find oxygen tanks would not have worked out as well as I would have hoped because I never did see any tanks. I had a lot of 'hindsight' moments to the point that I came up with my own adaptation of its traditional adage: *Hindsight is a know-*

it-all bitch.

One such know-it-all bitch moment was my denial about having COVID. I woke up on Easter Sunday, April 4, feeling nauseous with the first signs of sinus congestion. I forced myself to eat eggs for breakfast, and by some miracle, my nausea disappeared for that day. I started to take an over-the-counter medicine for my congestion, and I felt like I was getting better as the week continued. Based on the advice of my allergist nurse practitioner, I quit taking that medicine either on Wednesday or Thursday, thinking I was doing better.

By Friday, April 9, I was miserable and worse than I had been on Sunday. My nausea came back, and my brain was craving sleep. I begged one of my staff members to come work my afternoon shift, and I went home.

In another know-it-all bitch moment, I should have gone to EZ Care that day to figure out what was wrong sooner, but I was worried that I wouldn't be able to get myself home.

All of this denial was based on the notion that I had to have the most common symptom of COVID—a loss of taste and smell. Since I didn't lose either scent, my denial lead me to being a Typhoid Mary: COVID Edition for a full week before I was tested and diagnosed.

On one hand, my time in the ER went quickly as I kept busy with keeping family, friends, and the Edgar County Health Department up to speed with calls and texts, and all the tests that I had to undergo to see how badly COVID had ravaged my body.

I wasn't able to understand what all the medical professionals were telling me about the tests, and I wished that COVID restrictions hadn't kept Mom in the waiting room. She would have been able to help me understand what was going on, instead of me simply nodding to everything.

While there was a lot that I forgot, the CT scan stood out to me. Before this test, I was given something that would help show something in this test. The technician told me, "Now, you're going to feel like you're going to pee, but you're not. Don't move."

Everything she said was factual, but it was the biggest understatement I had ever heard. When they put me in the machine, it felt like my bladder decided to fill up right away and was ready to empty right then. I had to keep thinking to myself, *It's not real. Don't move. It's not real. Don't move.*

I was amazed when they didn't make me do it again because I was sure I had moved.

When I wasn't busy with testing or my phone, time did slow down. I tried to fill up the time with reading Philip Pullman's *The Subtle Knife.* As an avid reader, I love to spend my free time in between the pages of a book, but my lack of concentration made it hard for me to do my favorite past time lying in the ER bed.

Though the COVID pandemic was still in full swing, Terre Haute's Union Hospital had no beds available due to people having other ailments like heart attacks and strokes. The ER doctor spent many hours trying to find me a bed somewhere else. He finally found a bed at the Union Hospital in Clinton, Indiana.

When it became an issue of how to get me there, the doctor was determined that I would take an ambulance. I fought that a little because Mom kept reminding me in her calls and texts that I would be the one given that bill.

This was one of the scenarios that Mom stayed in Terre

Haute for—we were thinking that she could drive me instead of giving me another bill to pay when I made it home. If they would have given me an oxygen tank, I knew I would have been fine.

The doctor insisted on the ambulance, and I only stopped when he said that my insurance would pay because it was COVID-related. Believing that he knew what he was talking about, I stopped arguing.

Know-it-all-bitch moment: insurance didn't pay. That is only true when you have reached your insurance's deductible and out-of-pocket cost maximum. It would take a few more hospital bills before 'everything' was paid by insurance.

Once it was determined I was being moved to Clinton, the EMTs came while I was in the bathroom, preparing for the 20-minute drive ahead. As I was taking care of those bathroom matters, one of the EMTs gathered my stuff from my room.

I felt bad for him because I knew my bra was disgusting from all the sweating I had done earlier. And I was, of course, carting around one of the largest books ever made: the combined edition of *His Dark Materials* trilogy. I bet he was wishing he had let me go back to the room to collect my things.

When I was ready, the EMTs put me on the gurney, and we were off on a quiet ride to Clinton. I spent part of the ride texting, and the rest of it trying not to freak out that I didn't have a belt over the upper part of my body. Inertia was making its presence known, and I felt like my upper body was going to fall off the gurney.

Once we got to Clinton's Union Hospital, the EMTs took me directly to my room. They helped me into my bed with my oxygen tube hooked right up to the wall like it was at the ER. It was a hectic time with the EMTs leaving and nurses coming in to get me settled.

I had arrived right before the kitchen closed for the night, and a nurse kept hinting that I should order food right then if I wanted to eat that night. Though I wasn't hungry yet, I placed an order so I could eat when I was ready.

This was when I realized there was a silver lining to all this mess: because I could still taste, I was able to enjoy the hospital food.

While I did have food in the ER, I didn't take the time to really taste the food. I am not a fan of roast beef, but I ate every bite of it because I had been starving for hours. I had declared it delicious, but I couldn't describe the taste.

During my hospital stay, I kept thinking as if I was a food critic. If you should go to Union Hospital in Clinton, Indiana, get the chicken tacos and French fries. They were all magnificent, and I ordered the tacos twice, wishing I had had them sooner so I could have had them more often. Be aware of the pizza though. It tasted like cardboard, and it didn't agree with me either.

Besides the pizza not agreeing with me, my first night in the hospital was rough because my oxygen hose was short. It couldn't reach to the bathroom, which meant every time I needed to pee, I was on my own air power. Though I had a bathroom in my room, it was still as hard to walk there as it had been to walk down the hall at the ER.

The first time I went to pee, I was out of breath by the time I got to the door. Then I saw a measuring cup in the toilet. I promptly took that cup out and put it in the shower that I had no intention of touching. If I couldn't breathe while I peed, I wasn't going to pee in a cup.

Along with having to depend on my COVID-filled lungs on my pee trips, I kept having coughing fits throughout that first night, and my body kept undergoing violet spasms. I felt like my body was trying to get rid of mucus, but there was nothing to get rid of. The fits didn't get as bad as the one from Sunday night/Monday morning because I forgot that these happened. Old texts reminded me that these fits kept happening that first night.

The next morning, April 13, I received a tube extension at the suggestion of my night nurse, eradicating my breathless walks to the bathroom. I felt like this was one of the moments that proved God existed.

The measuring cup was found and replaced in the toilet that morning too. Feeling grateful for the tube extension, I resigned to use it because I was out of excuses. As I soon found out, peeing in that damn cup would have been impossible without that long tube because I had to hover over the toilet to do the paperwork to clean myself.

Having deemed the idea of hovering as dumb years ago when Mom tried to teach me to do it with public toilets, my knees, lungs, and I were not happy to find myself in a position where I had to hover. My doubts in God promptly returned.

The damn pee measuring cup was the bane of my existence all of Tuesday. Whenever any of the nurses came in, they didn't go check it. I was worried that I would come across as disrespectful if I said anything, but I did have to mention something when I was one pee trip away from making that puppy overflow.

Luckily, that blasted cup was not returned after it was emptied. Hallelujah!

When I first arrived at Clinton, I was put on fluids to

ensure I didn't get dehydrated. During my first conversation with the doctor on Tuesday morning, she mentioned that if I thought I could keep myself hydrated by drinking lots of water, she would take me off the fluids.

I think all the nurses on my floor regretted that decision because I kept every single one of them busy with bringing me water. Every hour or two, I was hitting my button to ask for water. I almost asked if there was a code or something I could do so they would know it was only water that I needed.

To make things more interesting, everyone who entered my room was supposed to put on gloves and a yellow cover over their scrubs to protect themselves from my COVID-riddled germs. Eric, my day nurse, called it his 'Big Bird outfit.'

At first, they would do that when my water was delivered. By the end of the first day and the rest of my time there, they rushed in quickly and got out once the water was on my tray.

Though our first conversation lead me to getting off fluids, there was something else the doctor told me that didn't sit well. She acted like I was going to die from COVID at any moment because I have insulin resistance. My body produces more insulin than it should to keep my blood sugar normal, and it could cause me to be a diabetic if left unchecked. That doesn't mean I'm a diabetic now.

Know-it-all-bitch moment: I didn't realize that my insulin resistance would have given me permission to get the vaccine early. I thought I was being a good citizen to allow vaccines to go to senior citizens and those with worse conditions than mine. I was 29.

How could I justify getting the vaccine under what I

thought would have been false pretenses?

If you were to judge by the Clinton doctor's reaction, I should have been shoving people in wheelchairs out of the way to get my shot.

She made me feel that she thought I was about to die on her, and I was thinking, *Lady, I clearly have way more confidence in you than you do.*

I knew as soon as I was on oxygen, I would be fine. Medical professionals had been fighting COVID for a year, and I didn't think I had let myself get too bad to where I was truly screwed. I only had a little COVID, a touch of pneumonia, and a butt-load of naïve optimism.

Even though the doctor was worried about my insulin resistance and treated me like a diabetic, she didn't put me on a diabetic diet restriction.

"Order whatever you want," she said.

You're kidding, right?

She had just lectured me about how they needed to be careful with me, but I had her permission to order all the cookies I wanted. Nothing that couldn't be fixed with a little insulin, right?

Coming from a long line of diabetics, I wasn't going to put myself in a position where I needed insulin. Besides, sweets were not that appetizing while I was sick.

As it turned out, there was something else that the doctor should have been worried about: I ended up having an allergic reaction to the medicine they gave me through my IV.

Normally, my medical allergic reactions have me itching my skin off, but my reaction caused the IV's entry point to be puffy, red, and painful.

In a know-it-all-bitch moment, I'm not sure any of the

medical staff or I understood that it was an allergic reaction until I called the first morning I was home to complain that my entire body was itching from the oral medicine the doctor gave me.

From the first dose, it hurt to have the medicine pumped into my vein, and the pain got worse with every dose. I complained every time so a nurse could adjust the speed that medicine was pumped into me. Each time, it took a little longer to get through a bag.

Almost a year later after this, my primary doctor told me that I couldn't have a Z-Pack anymore for sinus infections because it has the same medicine that gave me the reaction in the hospital.

Being by myself so much, I have a hard time remembering what I did. I still couldn't concentrate on reading, and it didn't help I was ticked with the ending of *The Subtle Knife*.

I did watch TV, and I have ingrained in my head that I watched *2 Fast, 2 Furious*. During the opening scene of the movie, Paul Walker is chasing a suspect, and I had never felt so much envy to watch someone run.

Those lucky, COVID-free bastards! I believed this thought to be so damn funny that I keep telling everyone about it.

After trying to piece together what else I did while at the hospital, I realized I was on my phone a lot. Of course, I spent a lot of time updating my parents, co-workers, and friends with how well I was doing, but I was also working a lot.

While I did have to work from home during my entire recovery, I logged the most hours during the week I was in the hospital. I was coordinating substitutes for my shift, managing the training for our new hire, and conveying messages from our executive director, Erin.

It didn't help that when I asked Erin whether or not I could tell my staff that I was one of the three staff members who tested positive, I misread her text. I thought she had told me not to say anything about what was happening to me because of fear of COVID-shaming and unintentional HIPPA violations. Reading over those same texts so I could write this story as factually as possible, I found that she did say I could tell the staff as a friend.

Know-it-all-bitch moment: I was upset with Erin, thinking she had told me to keep my condition a secret, and I didn't realize this was unnecessary and untrue until I reread the message more than a year later for this piece.

By Wednesday, April 14, my recovery was progressing, and it was time to see what I could do after the most exercise I had had was walking to the bathroom.

A physical therapist came to help me take a walk on the floor. He initially told me to walk to the nurses' station at the end of my hallway. It was a short walk that would have left me exhausted on Monday.

When he asked if I felt like going the long way, I nodded. I don't remember talking in the hallway, but I do know that I was confident that I could make the longer walk, and too stubborn to admit otherwise.

I didn't take in many details of what I saw, but I do remember seeing my doctor and Eric making their rounds, and they both cheered me on.

Back in my room, the therapist gave me a contraption that Google declared to be a Voldyne Incentive Spirometer. This thing has two tubes: a small, yellow piece of plastic is in the smaller tube that is supposed to be suspended in a clear window, and a larger tube has a white disk that the therapist told me he wanted me to make rise until it hit the 1,500 ml line by blowing into the attached hose at least 10 times an hour.

The therapist encouraged me to do this exercise a few times during the commercial breaks, and I would hit the goal. I didn't listen—I tried to hit that line 10 times during one commercial break. That may have been a little too aggressive because I wasn't close to hitting that line later in the hour.

The last hurtle to getting home was to get off the oxygen. The doctor told me on Wednesday that if they could get me off oxygen, I could go home on Thursday. I was excited, and I was telling everyone that I was getting close to leaving.

Looking back, I don't remember how the weaning worked. They may have lowered the oxygen level pumping through my tube, or they may have only had me take the tube off. I do remember that I was going without the oxygen tube by Wednesday evening, and it stayed off all night.

Since I was able to stop my dependence for my oxygen tube, the doctor made good on her promise to let me go home when she came to check on me Thursday morning, April 15. She told me a bunch of things, which I didn't fully understand at the time, and was thankful she put everything on paper.

She did mention having me go through pulmonary therapy because COVID had made my lungs act like I had smoked for 10 years though I had never touched a cigarette in my life. I thought this would be something I could start right away, but my primary doctor nixed that idea in our first telehealth call a week later with a quick, "You're not ready for that."

When I did finally get that testing completed, my pulmonary therapy consisted of me spending my lunch hours working out under medical supervision twice a week. I probably went longer than I needed to, but I had already decided that I would only stop when the therapists told me to. Turns out, as a self-pay participant, they couldn't tell me to quit.

The day of my discharge from the hospital must have been the same for everyone on the floor because poor Eric was overwhelmed with all the paperwork.

In fact, my muffin got temporarily lost in the shuffle. I think I may have accidently made the missing muffin a bigger deal than it was as I tried to track it down. They could have chucked it into my room as they walked past. My chances of catching it had improved compared to earlier that week.

As I was getting my stuff all gathered and getting dressed to go home on Thursday, I started looking around at the different toiletries left for me. There was all the things I should have been using for the last three days: toothpaste, tooth brush, comb, and deodorant.

I had seen the tub that had all this stuff in it earlier, but I couldn't focus enough to look through it, even after I got the tube extension. While I knew I really needed to use these products, for my own comfort and those of the medical staff, I couldn't. I didn't have the strength. I couldn't make myself care.

Thursday was the first time I felt well enough to pretend to be human, so that's when I finally investigated the tub. I brushed my teeth, brushed my hair, and put on deodorant all for the benefit of my parents and Eric.

Then I started taking things as if I had been staying in a hotel room. I knew that things that I had opened would be thrown away, so I didn't want to be wasteful. As for anything that I hadn't opened, I got a little grab-happy as if I didn't have my own toiletries at home.

Once everything was packed and I was ready to go with my discharge papers, all of my belongings felt like they had doubled. I was sure I didn't take that many things from the bathroom.

As I climbed into the wheelchair Eric brought, I piled everything into my lap, and the Get Well balloons sent by my aunt and uncle in Indianapolis kept blowing in Eric's face. I didn't think I could grab the strings without losing everything in my lap, but Eric handled it like a pro. I think he'd pushed a wheelchair while being attacked by balloons before.

Getting myself and my stuff into the car left me winded. The high of coming home started to dwindle as I exerted myself more and more. By the time I was home, showered, and undergone a quick haircut, I was exhausted. Mom made the comment that I was shuffling around like she does when her arthritis was bad.

That slow shuffle continued until I was physically able to take walks outside. My ability to breathe got better with the countless hours I practiced on my breathing exercise machine. Four months of pulmonary rehab shook out the last of the physical fatigue.

Though I was in the hospital for three and a half days, it was only the beginning to my recovery that I enjoy now. Until I bend down to tie my shoes—that still leaves me gasping.

About the Author
Kelly Nicholson

Being an academic overachiever, Kelly Nicholson graduated a year early from Eastern Illinois University with a Bachelor's degree in English and minors in creative writing and professional writing in 2013. Thinking that she would use her knowledge to become a fictional writer, her writing career has focused on nonfiction.

Despite claiming that she would never be a journalist, Kelly spent 20 months working as a general reporter for her hometown newspaper, the Paris Beacon-News, starting on a rainy day in 2014 where she had to sit in a corner and work for her first desk.

After hitting a wall of writer's block, she joined the Past-Forward Memoir Writing Group in 2017 and was a contributing author to the group's third book, *For the Record.*

Currently, Kelly is the Membership Director at the Paris Rec Center, where she enjoys being part of a not-for-profit that services so many people and helping people who want the Rec to be part of their fitness journey.

She has always loved books and writing, though her love for reading tends to get in the way of her love for writing. She is still semi-seriously contemplating starting a Reading Anonymous group.

This is the second time she had the privilege to contribute to an anthology.

I can't breathe.

Chapter 2

The Many Pearls of COVID

By Shelley Crouch

Pearls form when an irritant works its way into an oyster. As a defense, the mollusk secretes a liquid to coat the irritant. After layer upon layer of this coating, there is a beautiful pearl—beauty from irritation.

I gained many beautiful pearls during this challenging time of the COVID pandemic and the national quarantine. Although, they came after layer upon layer of irritation, some of which were very traumatic.

The Move

To set the scene for my journey, I should back up a few months to the beginning of 2020. On January 16th, my husband, John, and I, newly empty nesters, moved out of the three-story house in which we had spent the last eighteen and a half years into a smaller two-story home in town, only three blocks away from my mom.

We had just helped our youngest move an enclosed

trailer full of furniture up eight steps into an apartment in Indianapolis, a city two hours east of us. So, let's just say there was a lot of hauling boxes and furniture up and down flights of stairs in one month.

Anyone who has moved knows this is a stressful, exhausting, and ongoing task that we had labored toward for months. As a result, we were strained and drained, physically, mentally, and emotionally.

The Heart Attack

Five days later, on January 21st, my husband told me that his arms hurt, and he had pain across his back. This pain didn't seem out of place, considering he'd been moving heavy boxes for a month. However, he also complained that his jaw was sore. Even then, he noted that he'd probably been clenching it a lot due to the stress of moving.

My brain was beginning to put two and two together, and his face had a look of fear, not of back pain. I asked him if he thought I should take him to the hospital, and he didn't even argue. Now I was scared.

Our local hospital transferred him to a larger one, and I drove alone at midnight, completely overwhelmed and crying after forcing myself to stay calm in the ER with John. I listened to all the songs my husband had written and recorded on my CD player.

I was comforted by the sound of his voice, but my mind was racing. I pondered how my life would change in an instant if he didn't survive. My stomach tightened with the fear of losing him, and I realized I was holding my breath several times. I had to keep reminding myself to breathe.

The following day, the surgeon put two stents in John's heart, saying he had a 100% blockage in the widow maker artery and another 80% blockage. Just the name of the artery made me pause. I was so relieved the doctor told me *after* it was fixed and not before. John told me the pain left when the stent was in place, and he knew he was okay. He felt so much better.

Concerned about his dad, our oldest came right away from Texas with his wife and daughter and stayed with us the first week after John's heart attack. Our daughter-in-law is a nurse, and she bought groceries, made healthy meals, and tracked John's blood sugar. Our son went with John on his first walks for safety as he had dizzy spells while his body adjusted to his new medications. Our one-year-old granddaughter kept us all distracted and entertained.

In the days and months ahead, John started cardiac rehabilitation therapy (COVID restrictions would later shut it down before he finished) and began walking daily and eating healthy food. As a result, he lost weight, felt great, and had more energy than he'd had in years. It was scary, but he gained a healthier and happier version of himself. Almost losing him, I found myself appreciating him even more. Every day was a gift.

The Public Shutdown

Our darling toddler granddaughter and her parents returned for another stay in early March. The heart attack had been a reminder of how precarious life and family are. We had a great visit, but the news stations kept talking about a virus that started in China and was now in New York City and a few other cities.

Our Illinois governor announced a disaster proclamation on the second day of their visit because Illinois had eleven coronavirus cases. He banned large gatherings by the fourth day of their stay. He stated that Illinois schools would be closed for two weeks, effective Monday. The next day, he announced restaurants and bars would also be closed from indoor dining for two weeks. It seemed things were getting serious in a hurry.

The kids left for Texas, and I ordered groceries for my mom and us using Walmart's grocery pickup service I had used previously for convenience. It took me several hours and numerous texts to get a list from my mom. I finally got our order put in and went to bed. They emailed the following day that they suspended their pickup service due to too many orders. I couldn't believe it. I would have to go in.

I dropped John off at his cardiac rehab and went inside the Walmart to get groceries. There was an eerie feeling in the store that morning. The employees were stressed, as were many of the shoppers. People wanted to communicate with each other about this strange situation, but at the same time, people didn't want to get close enough to talk to each other.

These were the first days of this crisis, and most people didn't have face masks. There was a supposed shortage of face masks, and what was available was needed by hospital staff. The lady who checked out my groceries touched her mouth constantly and had round balls of saliva on the corners of her lips.

It would have been a disturbing sight in any

circumstance, but I found it particularly discomforting on this day. I could not find many things on my list due to the fury of shoppers the night before. We would have to make do with what we had.

Friends in China

"Teacher, do you have an N95?" my teenage student asked as our online class started. I assumed he was talking about some new handheld gaming device like the Nintendo 64 my kids had used. But he was showing me a specific type of facemask.

He wanted to make sure I had the safest one. I didn't even realize there were different kinds. This student was timid and rarely made small talk. It was touching that he cared enough about me to come out of his shell.

During the COVID pandemic, I was self-employed as an online ESL (English as a Second Language) teacher to mostly very young students in China. Early in the morning (their evening), I would meet with these precious children online to model correct pronunciation, the main goal of these classes.

Unlike American students who don't have such opportunities for a second language until high school, these kids learn English from preschool. But their teachers are usually Chinese, and their pronunciation of our language is often incorrect, causing parents to desire their children to learn correct pronunciation from an American.

These eager parents were usually by their side but off my screen. COVID-19 originated in China, so they were several steps ahead in responding to it. The Chinese moms of my students were horrified to see on the news that there was a shortage of face masks in America, so we were discouraged from buying them to save them for the frontline workers who needed them more.

My students and their mothers loved me, their one American friend, and these mothers were coming on the screen and trying, in their best broken English, to get my address so that they could ship face masks to me.

But, of course, face masks were not a new thing in China. They live and work so close together in their big cities that they often wear face masks, especially on public transportation, to avoid getting colds and flu from each other.

One mother wanted to show me how to wear a face mask because they had seen Americans on the news wearing face masks under their nose or even on their chin. She was concerned that we didn't know the correct way and that I could become sick.

I declined their offers for free masks because a friend had sewn a face mask for me, and we weren't leaving the house at the time. We were at the beginning of this crisis when we thought we'd only need them for a few weeks.

I couldn't bear to think of them spending the money when their children had to wear winter coats inside their apartments to keep warm—their families prioritizing supplemental education over a comfortable thermostat setting.

But this gesture, repeated by several moms, brought me to tears. Our short classes had never offered much time for small talk with mothers, but their concern for my safety meant more to them than their child getting a complete lesson.

Face Masks and Face-Offs

Many people refused to wear masks even when they were readily available in America. Unfortunately, face masks don't claim to protect the wearer from COVID. Instead, they intend to protect others from the wearer and a highly contagious disease you could carry without a single symptom.

I had no idea, initially, whether they helped. And wearing a mask was not something I enjoyed in the least. Still, if wearing it *might* save a stranger or loved one's life or even just make them feel safer, I was more than willing to sacrifice by wearing one, especially since it wasn't harmful to the numerous medical staff that had worn them for years.

My friends did not all share my views about face masks. One friend, who knew my husband was in a high-risk group, looked at me with disapproval when I answered my door wearing a mask. I'm not sure why this upset her, but perhaps because it implied that she should return the favor, and maybe she felt that violated her rights or harmed or inconvenienced her in some way.

I felt terrible for upsetting her, but I needed to do what I felt was in the best interests of others, especially the most vulnerable among us, *like my husband*, even if we might disagree about what that is. I may not have been helping anyone, but I wasn't harming anyone either. However, I felt sad that I might have hurt my friend's feelings. I do hope that she thought about our situation and understood.

Traditions Turned Upside Down

The continued quarantine began to affect more than just our day-to-day life. It affected our family traditions.

For example, when John's birthday rolled around on March 31st, we couldn't go out for supper or have family and friends over. But I still wanted John's birthday to be memorable. So, I made one of his favorite meals, something we call Friday Night Wings, and I made a homemade cake with homemade ice cream.

My mom walked over from her house, rang the bell, placed a gift bag on the doormat, and then went to stand further away when John opened the door. She sang Happy Birthday from the sidewalk, wished him a happy birthday, and walked back to her house. These were strange times indeed.

If I had thought of it, I would have had a piece of cake at the door for her to take home. But we were all still getting used to this, and honestly, we thought we would be back to normal soon, and we could just hold belated celebrations at that time. I saw many people have drive-by birthday parades for children.

Easter came as we were less than a month into this new pandemic lifestyle. Typically, we would have an Easter dinner at our home with whatever family could come. My mom always joined us. Often some of our kids would also be with us. However, this year was very different. First, we watched our church service online. I prepared communion to partake in virtually with our church family. Then, we had dinner for two at home. It all felt so strange.

After our small Easter meal, I packed up part of our dinner, put the containers in an Easter gift bag, drove to my mom's, set the bag on her doorstep, rang her doorbell, and then stepped back to her sidewalk. When she opened the door, she thanked me, and we wished each other a Happy Easter, and I went home to my husband. I felt so blue to be celebrating a holiday without family.

I knew it was tough on my mom. She was a very social person and struggled with loneliness living alone. Not getting to be with family on a holiday I knew would be depressing for her. So, I hoped that my small gesture helped her feel more connected in a time of such disconnect. And I think I succeeded because she texted me that evening, letting me know how much it meant to her.

The Casey's Corral

One cool thing I noticed was the different ways people found to experience old things in new ways. For example, before the pandemic, my husband and his other friends met at the local Casey's General Store every morning. But, of course, such loitering was not allowed during the quarantine.

A few weeks in, they came up with a new plan. They began to meet outside the building in an empty parking lot. They corralled their pickup trucks into a circle, and each sat on their tailgates and visited. I love all the creative ways people stay connected with friends and family. Humans are amazing.

Online Tech Support

One day, I had to provide tech support for my mom. Usually, I would go to her house to do this. This can be challenging if you are untrained to assist someone without seeing what the person asking the questions sees. It was the day of the deadline for submissions to our mutual writing group's collaborative memoir book. Though they were due at midnight, mom had waited until the last minute to submit them. The guidelines stated we should email our stories.

A few days earlier, my mom wrote hers out longhand in her messy cursive handwriting that *even she* could not decipher. Then she had the tedious task of transcribing her stories to her computer. She typed them out in Word but could not get them to send from there. I talked her through copying and pasting one of them to her email. It took me over an hour, and it reminded me why I went to her house to do this in the past.

Then she called me back frantic. One of her stories had disappeared entirely. I suspected she had clicked 'cut' instead of 'copy.' She was so distraught that it was difficult to coach her, but I asked if she could go to a blank page. When she finally did, I asked her to right-click and select 'paste.' I heard shouts of joy! Her story miraculously reappeared. She was jubilant, and I was relieved and exhausted.

Losing the Local Grocery Store

I typically preferred to buy from our local grocer. As local business owners for many years, we knew the importance of supporting one another. However, they did not carry many of the items we regularly purchased, so Walmart had become a more frequent stop than I wanted it to be.

Unfortunately, many other people in our town were also finding it more and more convenient to visit the big box stores instead of our local grocery store. As a result, our local IGA grocer was struggling more and more.

Now, with the pandemic, to lessen their exposure to

other people and thus their germs, folks wanted to purchase all their necessary items in one trip. But unfortunately, the lack of business was the final nail in the coffin, and they closed their doors for good on April 17th.

At the time, I remember that many local people lamented the loss. Our town had become a food desert. It was significant not only for the community but also for its most vulnerable members. They knew this loss would be felt even more by the older generation and those who didn't have a vehicle or gas money to get to other cities for food.

Losing a Loved One

The most significant loss I faced during COVID was made more devastating by the isolation of the quarantine. I lost my mother to an aortic aneurism. The whole story of this loss is found elsewhere in this book.

The public shutdown confounded nearly every protocol of comforting the bereaved—no funeral visitation, no visits from friends, no memorial service, and no hugs can happen in a time of social distancing. And my mom's death came just six weeks into it when the risks and restrictions were the most severe. It was devastating.

Creativity Abounds

One of the pearls I discovered in this time of significant loss was using art as a form of therapy for my grief. It made me feel connected to my mom. This discovery of art as therapy came when I suddenly had newfound time to work creatively. This free time led to creative pursuits in every direction.

I learned to watercolor paint and made numerous board books for my granddaughter. And now, I am branching out by making fabric portraits, acrylic paintings, and mixed media works. In addition, I have entered several art shows.

I also took lessons and learned to play the bass guitar and have been able to accompany my husband on a few outdoor music gigs as they finally opened again. It's fun to be up on stage together. It has added another layer to our relationship to make music together.

Additionally, my writing group continued to meet on Zoom, and now, with my calendar primarily bare, I had time for more writing. The more I wrote, the more I wanted to write. It's addictive.

As a result, I am working on a book combining the memoirs I found amongst my mother's papers and my memoirs. The process of working on this has been such a joy. I also picked up an old fiction writing project, breathing new life into it.

Our local yarn shop started an online class called The First Stitch Club, and I have learned to knit. I was able to give family members homemade knitted gifts at Christmas. I couldn't believe how nice they looked. I was so proud of myself.

I intend to remember that this burst of creativity and creative projects came from an open calendar. If I let it get full again, it's apt to push my creative pursuits back to the back burner.

~~~~

THE CHAOS OF COVID

Discovering New Locales

Once restaurants could open with new restrictions, we ventured out. We were thrilled to discover places to eat outside. We found a lovely restaurant that was new to us in a nearby town with two tables on the sidewalk. If we got there early, which is no problem for our age group, we could eat at one of them. We had never been before, but we loved the food and the staff, and we still go every week, but now we can sit inside.

There is another restaurant in that neighboring town with patio seating overlooking the lake. We loved having dates there. The view was spectacular, and the food was delicious. We were enjoying nature more than ever before, and it was lovely.

We often picked up food from our favorite Mexican restaurant and ate it at a nearby park. It was fun to do different things we had never done before. We saw the world through new eyes.

We found a new place to hike by another lake and often went there. It had a nice wide path, so you could easily walk safely, even when other hikers were out. We did more hiking in general since we wanted to get out of the house, and this was a reasonably safe activity, even for someone at risk of COVID.

Another thing we started doing at this time was watching movies at home instead of going to the theater. We liked this more than we thought we might. Every Saturday night found us watching a movie and eating freshly popped corn.

A bonus was the ability to stream new movies because they couldn't show them at the theater, but they needed to get them out. In addition, our new movie night was much less expensive than it used to be.

Different Ways to Travel

As the two-week quarantine became seemingly endless, we were desperate to see our granddaughter. Babies grow and change rapidly, and we were missing the early stages of her life. Our daughter-in-law didn't want to put John at risk by having us travel to Texas, which was spiking with COVID cases, and our granddaughter didn't travel well without getting carsick.

So, in August, we decided to rent an Airbnb home halfway between our houses. We would do a grocery pickup on the way in, and we would only be exposed to each other. We had a wonderful visit with our grandbaby and her parents. It was great for us to escape our homes for a while. We were all starting to feel cooped up.

New Form of Litter

On our walks, John and I started noticing more litter everywhere. I guess part of the reason was that, for a while, the people who generally would pick up trash might not have been working or only worked in areas where they would not be exposed to other people.

The litter we were seeing was disposable and even non-disposable facemasks. These masks were everywhere, mainly outside the doors of buildings. The front yard of the high school was plastered with them. We noticed they were even hanging from the trees. After a long day of wearing masks in class, I suppose the students shot them like slingshots as soon as they passed the school's front doors.

Turnabout: Kids Worrying About Their Parents

You typically think about parents worrying about their kids, especially regarding illnesses. However, COVID found many kids of all ages worrying about their parents.

I know that I was worried about my mom while she was still alive, dissuading her from non-essential visits for physical therapy and making sure she would wear a mask to her doctor's appointments and other necessary errands.

I remember trying to talk my independent mother out of going to the store for grocery shopping and letting me order online. She couldn't figure out the technology to do it online, but she didn't want to be a burden to me.

When our middle child traveled from New York City in July of 2020, he and his girlfriend took many precautions to protect us. They stood in an hours-long line to get tested before leaving, drove instead of flying, went directly to our cabin, and wouldn't see us unless we were all outdoors and far apart.

They tested four days after arriving and then again eight days after arriving, and only then would they be indoors with us. And even then, they took their temperature and oxygen each time upon coming into the house.

He couldn't stand the possibility of bringing the virus from New York City to our small town or infecting his dad with all his comorbidities. Of course, we appreciated his caution, but I must admit, it seemed odd that our kids were protecting us after years of protecting them. And I knew of many other kids, old and young, who were terrified of causing their parents' deaths.

I also remember that when they came again at Christmas, his girlfriend called her mom to visit and found out that her mom had been able to be vaccinated that day due to her job in public mental health. She wept with relief after she hung up the phone with her mother.

Return to a New Normal

We are both vaccinated, and most places are back to business as usual for the most part, but we are different people than before. In so many ways, I believe we have become better people.

I am a more creative person now and purposeful in my relationships, with a new appreciation for the benefits of a clear calendar. I hope I remember this. Also, I have a renewed compassion for those who live alone. But mostly, I am thankful for how I've grown. What beautiful pearls I have harvested from this unwanted irritation.

About the Author
Shelley Crouch

Shelley Crouch hails from Casey, Illinois, home of 3,000 people and a dozen World's Largest things, two of which she can see from her living room window.

Living in the home of the Big Things in a Small Town, Shelley has big dreams in a small town.

Besides being a writer/author, she also fancies herself an artist/illustrator. She has written and illustrated four nonfiction board books for toddlers: *Pond Life, 2020, My Bug Book, 2020, Texas Wildlife, 2020, and My Bird Book, 2021,* filled with simple watercolors and text.

She is working with Crystal Heart Imprints Publishing to make these available in a more economical paperback form. Until then, you can check them out through the interlibrary loan program of the Illinois Heartland Library System.

Shelley was recently part of Past-Forward's Memoir Writer's collaborative memoir collection, *For the Record,* published by CHI in November 2021.

She is currently working on a collection of her, and her late mother's memoirs tentatively titled, *Like Mother, Like Daughter: Memories Across the Generations.*

And to keep things interesting, she is crossing over to fiction. She is working on a mystery for middle-grade children titled, *Only the Dog Knows,* illustrated with simple pen and ink drawings, and an illustrated storybook for preschoolers, *Emily's Moon,* with prints from acrylic paintings. She plans to publish all these works in 2023-2025.

Shelley has been married for thirty-eight years to John Crouch. He is the most encouraging and supportive husband, and she is most grateful for that. He is a sixth-generation farmer and guitar-playing singer-songwriter with two CDs out. They have three talented children and two delightful grandchildren.

So thankful to have found CHI Publishing, Shelley enjoys the incredible support they provide to their writers throughout the process.

Chapter 3

Two years later:
Rising From the Ashes of All that Once Was

By Lynne Fireheart

Friday, March 13, 2020, was the last day of normalcy for this family of four. Little did we know as we hunkered down in those early days of sheltering in place that we would go through multiple iterations of school over the course of a year and a half; that my leisurely part-time massage therapy career would have to transform into a serious full-time hustle; and that the very fabric of our family would be ripped apart.

School

When the governor announced his Shelter in Place order, we all thought school would be closed for about three weeks. My son, Nova, was in 3rd grade, in a self-contained emotional and behavioral program, while my daughter, Neve, was in a 2nd grade general education classroom. Both children have additional support needs and had Individualized Education Plans (IEP) in place.

At first, "school" comprised weekly Choice Boards: six rows of different activities or assignments arranged in columns. For Neve, the columns were labeled by days of the week, and she had different boards for Physical Education (PE), Math, Reading, Music, Social-Emotional Learning, etc. Nova had just the one board, with columns labeled by subject.

Both children had additional boards for the Social Work, Occupational Therapy, or Speech services they were receiving in school. All these Choice Boards were printed out and available for pickup on Tuesday, March 17, 2020. I remember picking up the packets and immediately feeling concerned about the heft of the envelopes. All that paper. All those expectations.

I took a deep breath, and did what I could, in my own way.

Using up quite a bit of chalk, I drew a huge Snakes & Ladders grid on the driveway. We then played the game by physically moving from one square to another, running down the snakes, and running up the ladders.

Who could say we weren't doing PE (physical activity in general), Math (adding and subtracting numbers to determine which square to move to) and Social-Emotional Learning (playing a board game, and taking turns)? So what if those specific activities were not on any Choice Boards?

I also created a scavenger hunt that forced us out of the house to walk around the neighborhood (PE, physical activity), count cars (Math, tallying) and adding house numbers (Math, addition). We could not go to any playgrounds, as they were closed to the public.

Then the in-person learning moratorium was extended to the end of the school year, resulting in more, overwhelming, Choice Boards available for pick up every couple of weeks. Teachers introduced weekly or biweekly online sessions, using Zoom or Google Meet, that strove to impart some learning while also keeping classmates in touch with each other.

In addition to trying to be 'teacher,' I was also occupational therapist, speech pathologist, and social worker. I would email photos of the occasional completed work to the relevant personnel, and they would respond positively and encouragingly. No one pointed out that I was not submitting all the required work. I believe we all were doing the best we could in such unprecedented conditions.

We happened to have two small tables and matching chairs that the children had not quite outgrown. These were set up in the living room and cordoned off with blue electric tape on the floor to denote the 'school' area. My laptop was used by both children for their online needs. We could manage, but it was apparent that if remote learning continued, there needed to be a better arrangement, equipment-wise. I needed access to my laptop too!

The last week of school was bittersweet. So glad school was over for now, but also filled with uncertainty as to what school would look like come August. When would Nova and Neve get to physically be with their friends and classmates again?

Then came summer. Nova was eligible for, and attended, a five week online Extended School Year (ESY).

He would pay more attention to changing the background, muting and unmuting the microphone, toggling the camera on and off, and pasting links to various videos in the chat box, than he would to the lesson itself.

At least the summer packet included numerous hands-on projects that Neve and I worked on, with Nova tangentially involved. I truly don't know if Nova got anything out of those five weeks.

When school started up again in mid-August 2020, it was still in remote learning mode. Every student was issued a Chromebook. Nova was now in 4th grade, and Neve in 3rd.

Delivery of lessons evolved: days were very scheduled and run using Google Classroom and Google Meet as if the children were in class. More packets with even more papers and expectations were to be picked up and used. These papers started piling up, overflowing beyond the blue electric tape on the floor. The clutter grew and grew, as less and less required work was actually completed every day.

Nova continued to struggle to focus beyond the computer settings, while Neve would self-direct her learning through educational websites rather than pay attention in 'class.'

I worked with the children's teachers and the home interventionist, advocating for lowered expectations on Nova and Neve's attendance and participation. By this time, the family was in disarray, and I was barely getting one foot in front of the other: honestly, as long as both were sitting in front of the screen, that was good enough for me.

A month or so after school started, the school district

required a decision: go in-person or stay remote. Since neither parent was working, we chose to stay remote and continue sheltering in place as much as possible. This wreaked havoc on Neve's class arrangement.

She was one of the few reassigned to a totally different online teacher based in a different school altogether, as most of her classmates returned to school in person. Neve continued to not participate as expected but was learning in her own way.

For Nova, we tried a few different tactics to get the learning delivered effectively. His teacher even stayed late after school so she could do 1:1 online time with him. This did help a little, but Nova continued to struggle, and this wasn't a sustainable arrangement.

In November, there was another opportunity to shift to in-person learning after the winter break, but we decided to stay remote as we continued to prioritize sheltering in place.

The school district was clear, the decision would be binding. We all did the best we could remotely, but I confess the packets of work were going untouched most of the time. I felt bad for all that wasted paper.

It didn't help that in mid-December 2020 we put our house on the market, so my priority was first prepping the house for listing, followed by totally emptying it for sale almost immediately after. School attendance and performance had to take a back seat.

Picture moving from a huge 5-bedroom 3.5-bathroom house into a tiny 2-bedroom 1-bathroom apartment. One child had to "do" school in the living room, and the other in their shared bedroom. Both continued to not participate the way they were expected to.

I continued to attempt to enforce expectations, while also dealing with all the things related to the end of the marriage. We were all not in a good space mentally, and it showed in the children's school participation and our mental health.

After winter break in January 2021, it became increasingly apparent Nova was better off doing in-person schooling. At first, I negotiated for in-person Occupational Therapy and Social Work services for the children. It wasn't enough, as actual learning was still not happening.

I asked, and thankfully permission was granted–Nova could return to school! Since we were no longer living in the school district, however, Nova wouldn't qualify for the transportation he would have otherwise received by virtue of being enrolled in the emotional and behavioral program. I, with Neve in tow, would need to drive him to and from school.

Nova's classroom was already set up in such a way that social distancing was not an issue. I had feared he would refuse to wear his mask, as he complained of not being able to breathe in it, but he acclimatized soon enough to the point where he was wearing his mask even at home after school. I often had to remove the mask when he was asleep!

Neve was still remote at this time. Once her brother was dropped off at school, we turned right back around so she would, in theory, start her school. She continued with in-person Social Work services, and I also arranged for her to spend therapeutic time with the emotional support dogs they had at school.

As I mentioned earlier, Neve was doing self-directed learning via numerous educational websites most of the time. Then came time for a district-wide assessment: I found myself advocating for reasonable accommodations and expectations, and I believe she managed to meet the strict requirements. It felt like an uphill battle, however, and when Neve's attendance started getting flagged, I threw in the towel.

I asked for Neve to also be allowed back in-person. This was a huge ask, but thankfully the school could accommodate it. Neve returned to school after Spring Break, in March 2021. She and her classmates socially distanced in class, during lunch and at recess; they sanitized their hands often and took numerous mask breaks outside daily.

Around this time we moved again, to an apartment in the correct school district. Unexpected bonus: not only did Nova qualify for transportation again, but Neve was approved to ride along as well since there was space on the bus, even with socially distanced seating arrangements.

Of course, things were not hunky dory in school. While Nova's reentry happened seamlessly, Neve was struggling. The school and personnel, stretched to the limit by everything, had great difficulty with Neve's physical aggression, verbal aggression, and elopements.

It was all understandable behavior for a child both living through unprecedented pandemic times and processing the end of their family as they knew it. The end of the school year could not come soon enough.

Over the summer, Nova once again attended his ESY, this time in-person, transported to and from by bus. School continued to enforce social distancing, masks, and hand sanitizing.

In mid-August 2021 Nova entered 5th grade, and Neve

entered 4th grade, both in-person. The school allowed volunteers once more, and I was able to help out at the school library again. The duties had changed a little. It used to be that volunteers were required throughout the day, checking in books, shelving them, and also manning the check-out process for each class.

Now all classes were to return their books first thing in the morning, and volunteers were only there for an hour to check books back in and shelve them. The students would check out their books themselves. This new system seems to be working well.

Two years after we started sheltering in place, school seems to have settled back into a new normal.

Work

Prior to the Shelter in Place order being issued, I was playing at being a licensed massage therapist. I worked out of my colleague's office, sharing a room with a reflexologist. I would work twice a week, while the kids were in school. I would schedule a leisurely 30-minute gap between clients, when most others had 5 to 15 minutes. I had a handful of clients and was taking my time building my client base.

Then in mid-March 2020 all thought of massage was put on hold as I navigated the school situation. My fellow massage therapists just plain could not ply their trade: as a hands-on profession that worked up close and personal with clients, bodyworkers certainly could not maintain the required six feet of distance.

In addition, the powers that be did not consider massage therapy an essential service, even for massages provided within a healthcare setting. Don't get me started on how vital massage therapists could have been in addressing the stress faced by frontline personnel.

Instead, we were lumped together with hairdressers and estheticians, and had to put up with our places of work being referred to as massage parlors, with all the baggage that comes with that term.

At this time, some bodywork professionals were able to pivot to remote, online offerings, mainly those who provided Reiki and other energy services. Numerous free courses popped up: if you were stuck at home at least you could dive into some new knowledge, right?

The optimist in me signed up for many such courses. However, I quickly found I had no capacity to absorb anything as I struggled with energy and priorities.

I had received certification as a breath coach on March 13, 2020, as the world ground to a halt. I thought I had the perfect online offering, but as a not just small but tiny business owner I struggled to get the word out.

I did some Facebook lives, scheduled some Zoom sessions, created a Facebook group, but there was no traction. I stopped trying after a month and poured my energy into mom and school mode.

In mid-May, clarification arrived: Massage therapists were deemed essential only if they worked for a doctor or physician who prescribed massage therapy as part of the patient's treatment plan. As such, massage therapists needed their clients to produce a doctor's order before working on them.

At the end of May, guidelines eased up, but massage sessions were limited to 30 minutes, and all parties needed to be masked. A few weeks later, the time restriction was lifted. Through all these changes, I remained at home navigating the end of school, and summertime survival mode.

By the time July rolled around, however, I was ready to start up again. I had the opportunity to use my colleague's room on a random Saturday: despite having two rooms, only one room could be used at a time due to occupancy restrictions. I also started seeing clients in Springfield one weekend a month. The children's father would manage the children while I was out.

Determined to offer massage services safely, I implemented a few COVID-specific protocols. I bought an air purifier that filtered particles a minimum of 0.1 microns, the size of the COVID-19 virus.

To address cross-contamination, I stored individual sets of massage linens in their own extra-large Ziploc bags and obtained an easy-to-sanitize shower cap-like vinyl cover for the massage table. To address not wearing a mask while face-down, I had clients breathe into a large pillowcase attached to the face cradle—I'm surprised only one client balked at the claustrophobic set-up.

I continued with the 30-minute gap between clients. I wiped everything down with a sanitizer between clients.

Things were going pretty smoothly, until a resurgence at the end of October 2020 resulted in stricter guidelines, with massage once again only 'allowed as deemed necessary by a medical provider.' By this time, I was essentially a single parent with no one to watch the children.

I stopped working and didn't keep tabs on the changing requirements. I know things got stricter before restrictions eased up again.

After a ten-month hiatus, in August 2021, I dipped my toe back into the massage waters, planning to work on Saturdays, using a different friend's office. I had found a couple of babysitters over the summer and hired them to watch the children while I worked. It was so nice to be massaging again, and my clients were also delighted to have me back. I maintained the same protocols as before.

However, it became obvious very quickly that the small work income and large babysitting costs were just not sustainable. I decided to go all in and rent a room of my own, and work while the children were in school.

I found a suitable room, and moved my equipment and furniture in October 2021, confident I would get plenty of referrals and overflow from my fellow massage therapist colleagues.

I was mistaken.

After a few months of sporadic local clients, I had to admit that I needed a guaranteed income that my private work was just not providing at the time. My plans to become a life coach were also facing delays as I couldn't find the focus to complete the courses I'd purchased.

I joined a massage salon in January 2022 and took to the work like a fish to water, finally truly in my element. My initial two-day schedule filled up easily. I added a third day and worked my way up to a higher commission level.

I now have little spare time while the children are in school. I continue to cultivate and serve some clients in my private room on the other two days of the week. The children stay with their father every other weekend, allowing me to massage in Springfield one weekend a month without needing to worry about childcare.

Two years after we started sheltering in place, I am no

longer playing: I am working hard to make a living wage and support my family as a licensed massage therapist.

Family

Prior to the Shelter in Place order being issued, I already led a pretty solitary life as a parent to two children with atypical, additional needs. I think only fellow special needs parents can relate to the isolation that creeps in as you realize your children can't handle birthday parties, Tae Kwon-Do lessons, even playdates without numerous difficulties erupting. You find yourself avoiding more and more social activities other families might attend without a second thought. It worked for my introverted personality, though.

I had precious kid-free time when Nova and Neve were in school; once they came home, I was on mom duty until bedtime, which could be a huge battle in itself. After that, my husband and I would numb out in front of the television until we retired for the night a few hours later.

The isolation that happened when the world shut down, however, was very different. We could no longer go out, even to a park: the house became my entire world. The basement became where we would hang out most of the day, when not in "school."

We had a wading pool filled with sliced pool noodles: jumping into this provided great sensory input. Nova and Neve built an obstacle course with the furniture available. We played pool noodle baseball. The children actually used the foosball table. We watched a whole bunch of GoNoodle videos for some exercise and amusement. We even played balloon tennis with flyswatters as racquets.

Once the playgrounds reopened, I took the children there often, and for the longest time I was vigilant about making us use hand sanitizer when we got in the minivan to go home and having us all change into fresh clothes as soon as we reentered the house.

The marriage was already in poor shape: we were both unhappy but struggled to get anywhere when attempting to address it. Once we started sheltering in place, however, it felt like a bright hot spotlight was shining down on the elephant in the figurative room of our marriage. Cracks kept appearing, deepening, widening, until one day in August 2020 it exploded in spectacular fashion.

Not just mere waves, but tsunami after tsunami of anger, grief, rage and hurt swept over me. His actions tore open deep ancestral wounds of abandonment and betrayal I hadn't known existed. I had no choice but to work through them, one painful day at a time.

Thanks to all the inner work I had already been doing since 2014, through Shamanic Breathwork, mental health therapy, and many things in between, I knew not to take on that which wasn't mine. Didn't make it an easy experience.

Breaking cycles is not for the faint of heart, and it has been quite a journey to the other side of the grief. Rather than picking up the pieces, I forged my own new path as a functionally single parent. The isolation was worse now that I was flying solo. Asking anyone to watch the children while I ran important kid-free errands felt like such a huge ask to make of anyone.

Then came the need to sell what should have been our forever home. The December 2020 move to the 2-bedroom 1-bathroom apartment required huge adjustments of the three of us. We could hear our many neighbors around us, and they surely heard Nova's many screams and stomps.

We still remember when all three of us needed to use the sole bathroom at the same time, and we had to hold it in and take turns. Once the weather warmed up, it was apparent the wall-mounted air conditioning unit was only capable of cooling down the living room, everywhere else was warm and humid.

I wasn't keen on moving again so soon, but we needed a 3-bedroom 2-bathroom ground floor apartment with central air if we were going to survive. It took many trips to multiple apartments before we found a suitable one. We moved again in April 2021, and we agree we've found our long-term rental home, for now.

While all that was happening, I also needed to keep the household going. Remote learning still needed to happen, as described previously. Groceries still needed to be shopped for, now by me with Nova and Neve in tow. Meals still needed to be prepped, served, and cleaned up after. Laundry still needed to be washed, dried, folded, and put away. In other words, life still needed to go on.

I don't really know how we made it to the end of that school year, but we did.

We spent the summer of 2021 recovering from all that had happened. I am still learning to make myself a priority in healthy ways. When Neve found herself crying at certain songs, I knew she was finally allowing herself to feel again.

Similarly, when Nova took to the sand tray and acted out two teams warring over a misunderstanding, I knew he, too, was finally starting to process the trauma of the past year. Only then could I be certain there was healing

THE CHAOS OF COVID

Two years after we started sheltering in place, we are now a divorcing family of three navigating unchartered waters, together.

About the Author
Lynne Fireheart

Lynne Fireheart grew up with her nose stuck in books by Enid Blyton, Hugh Lofting, Stephen King, and Piers Anthony and currently cites Alex Bledsoe, Neil Gaiman, Patrick Rothfuss, and Brené Brown as her favorite authors (one of these is not like the others).

Since becoming a mother, Lynne has struggled to find the time and energy to read and write consistently but continues trying to get back into the groove of 2006 where she read over 80 books, ran multiple personal blogs, and started her novel about a Malaysian vampire in Chicago.

In the meantime, she advocates fiercely for her children in school, works industriously as a massage therapist, and dives determinedly into Shamanic Breathwork, priestess initiations, and other self-discovery practices.

In what little spare time she has, Lynne enjoys tennis, Indian and Thai food, and police procedural tv shows. She is also a fan of the Oxford comma.

Lynne may be contacted at lynnefireheart@ gmail.com.

Chapter 4

Existential Crisis:
Unmasking the Shadow, Embracing the Truth

By Tiffany McBride

<u>Skeletons</u>

We're all a little mad here
Hoping our skeletons disappear
Never to be seen
Hidden behind the screen
So we think....
Until the bones begin to stink
The stench will eat at you
Something you need to attend to
Before it haunts your dreams
And your psyche screams
The bones weep for their structured form
Let them out to transform
To be whole again
Otherwise, you're only a flimsy mess of skin
- Tiffany McBride

The Prelude: The Portrait

Wow, I don't even recognize that person anymore.

I held a picture I recently had found from a month after it all began. The image was of a woman, her complexion light, young, and beautiful. Her eyes were bright, full of spunk and life, with a cheeky grin and her energy full of compassion.

The passion in her eyes reflected the power and fire she embraced. She was out to conquer the world and save the day. She was warm and sweet by the softness you could see on her face. Her hair was colored and full of body from her long, beautiful dreads. A total hippy.

Deep grief suddenly welled up inside of my chest. Sadness and gloom crept in, then the dullness and the sick feeling in my stomach. I looked up at the new reality in the mirror, now two years later.

My complexion was now dull and discolored. My face aged, and more silver strands appeared around my crown. A shadow of exhaustion and weariness hung over my head. My eyes were small and tired. My expression was swollen due to the stress and inflammation, adding weight to my face.

I gained about 40 lbs. from all of the ass sitting and the convenience of door dash and Amazon. I looked like someone I didn't know but knew intimately well. I couldn't pinpoint it, but I could tell that my spirit and light had disappeared. That woman from the picture was gone.

I had escaped the virus for two years by isolating myself and staying reserved in my tiny apartment. However, I decided to risk traveling internationally during the worst outbreak of COVID-19 the U.S. had ever seen in the winter of 2021/22. I had gotten it when I headed back home from Mexico. COVID wasn't as destructive in the beginning, as the months that followed.

My greatest fear had come true – I began suffering from the chronic symptoms of long haul COVID. After contracting the virus, I struggled with chronic sinus pain, headaches, fatigue, sore muscles, brain fog, short-term memory loss, deep depression, nose bleeds, and sinus infections in the months that followed.

The fear of losing my intelligence or brain capacity to function led me to my doctor's office. He had drawn blood and tested for several things. The level of inflammation in my body was very high.

As my doctor showed me the charts, he looked at me and said, "I'm worried about your brain, Tiff."

I smirked as if I knew, "I'm worried about my brain, too, Doc."

That was it. After the previous two years of political unrest, violent protests, psychological warfare, unemployment, change, depression, loss, loneliness, division, separation, global trauma, war, existential crisis, and striving to keep my recovery and sobriety, I had finally lost my mind. It felt like the grand finale of some Twilight TV series, the first episode titled *Friday the 13th*.

1ˢᵗ *Episode: Friday the 13th*

It was Friday the 13th of March 2020 when the panic spread across the United States concerning a deadly virus sweeping the entire world. The President had declared a nationwide emergency. The Center for Disease Control and Prevention placed travel restrictions and canceled flights and shipments. U.S. states began to shut down and mandated people to stay home to quarantine.

No one knew how long the social distancing mandate would last; many were hopeful that it would disappear in a few months. However, it became more surrealistic as mask-wearing was mandated, and social distancing guidelines continued to extend for months. I began to feel like I was living in a dream or cinematic movie; reality was just a wake-up call away.

Businesses and schools were shut down, and only the main essential places were open with restrictions. People were constantly afraid of losing their financial income, loved ones, and rights.

By May 2020, the U.S. had surpassed 100,000 related deaths to COVID. There was a shortage of medical supplies throughout the entire globe. The U.S. unemployment rate was 14.7%, the worst rate since the Great Depression.

With 20.5 million people out of work, hospitality, leisure, and healthcare industries took the most significant hit. It affected low-income and minority workers the most. Fortunately, I worked as a clinical therapist with a choice to move to virtual counseling with clients.

It was very stressful to be on the invisible front lines of the mental health crisis, helping clients maintain their sanity and my own.

I lived alone and when everything shut down, so did my entire social life. I enjoyed the loneliness and solitude for a few months until it became too much. I was working online during the day and trying to go to class and write papers for my Doctorate program in the evenings.

It felt like I was sitting all day and staring at a screen. And when I wasn't staring at a screen, I was staring at my walls. My apartment wasn't in the best location; it was run-down and smelled like mildew. There wasn't a washer and dryer available, and the walls were an ugly brown color. The carpet was also brown and worn down.

I tried to make it homey and comfortable as best as I could. However, eventually, the brown walls and carpet seemed to enclose me. The air conditioner was a piece of shit and only worked half the time. My plants kept dying by the end of May, and it became too hot in the apartment to keep them alive.

I don't think I was processing anything with how busy I stayed with work and school. I was trying to disassociate myself from it. A sense of denial; of trying to keep the rose-colored glasses on. Good vibes only, love and light bullshit. Until May 25th, 2020. Then the 2nd episode of the series began.

2nd Episode: Existential Crisis

Existential Crisis is a term used in psychotherapy or psychology. It refers to the inner conflicts one goes through when one begins to question their identity, their existence in the world, humanity, and the impression that life lacks meaning. Existential Crises can be accompanied by a time of intense difficulty, trouble, or danger, such as a global pandemic.

During these times, a person can develop high levels of anxiety, stress, depression, difficulty functioning cognitively, negative attitude, emotional pain, despair, hopelessness, guilt, loneliness, a loss of personal value, and the constant reflection on one's mortality. Many people express their existential dread through utilizing addictions, being anti-social, or having compulsive behaviors.

On May 25th, 2020, a person of color named George Floyd was murdered on social media by a police officer. His death began a massive uprising of pain and trauma, and the force of the Black Lives Matter protests and the hidden violence of racism in our country. His death brought so much anger into my body that I could barely contain it.

It uprooted emotions I had never felt before. By June, I had a horrible existential crisis and mental breakdown. I contemplated quitting my job and had a panic attack while my supervisor was on the phone. She suggested I take some time off and see how I felt afterward.

The skeletons start to peek out of the darkest closets if you sit still enough.

When I took off from work, I was trying to finish up my summer doctorate classes and failed miserably. I never got an F on a final paper or was threatened with plagiarism in my whole academic life. There was no compassion from my professors, and I rebelliously quit school.

I began to act out recklessly and impulsively, drinking hard liquor alone (not a good idea), smoking tons of weed, and acting out sexually. I had recently had my heart broken before the world shut down in March, so that grief began to come to the surface.

I had to face the shadows I was trying to avoid. I covered the mirrors in my apartment because I didn't particularly appreciate looking at my reflection. I pulled out my dreads like I had a psychotic episode and burned them in a fire.

It took me 20 days to pull them out, and after the 20th day, I cried bitterly. I loved my dreads, but I couldn't stand it anymore. The hippy was dying in me, and the darkness crept in more and more. The world's hate re-triggered my old wounds, and they began to bleed out.

Even though I had gone back to work, I needed help by August. I realized I was an addict and mentally ill, and I needed to seek out some professional assistance. I began working with a therapist and sought out a spiritual recovery group and started working through my skeletons one by one.

3rd Episode: The Skeletons in the Closet

Before the pandemic, I lived two lives. One was of perfectionism, and one was of secrets.

Camouflage so I can feed the lie that I'm composed
I've got a monster inside me
That eats personality types.
                    - Halsey

I was good at first impressions. I could show you a mask of trinkets, accomplishments, and entertaining hobbies; see all my degrees, I got 20. I could compose myself as someone who had it together and knew it all. My performance and image were the only things that held my sanity together by threads.

My beauty and charm allowed me to be adored by men and fed the lie that I was good enough. I could be whatever you wanted me to be because I had perfected the art of people-pleasing and codependency.

Only those close to me knew that I struggled with mental health, instability, and substances. But even then, I would keep people at a distance, and didn't have any long-term relationships, because once they figured me out, I had moved on. I often just played the healer among friends and didn't get vulnerable about myself.

Did anyone really know me? Did I even know myself? Who was I, really?

By the Fall of 2020, I began dismantling the masks I hid behind. I could be whatever anyone wanted me to be. I could form myself to help others feel more comfortable. I had so many masks I could find one that fit each person I encountered. So many acts to choose from.

I learned to have each one accessible at all times. It was okay when someone said I was doing something wrong because I could change my mask to fit their need. If I wasn't behaving in a certain way, I had a show for that.

I had worn so many masks at this point in my life that I wondered who the actual person was underneath. As I took off the masks, I realized that I was tired, depleted, and inflamed from all the pretending. I just wanted to be comfortable. I was curious if I could take the masks off and keep them off. I was afraid of making other people uncomfortable, fearful they wouldn't accept or like me if I exposed my truth. The truth under all the masks.

4th Episode: Unmasking the Shadow

My very first mask was the one of codependency. I explored my past traumas from childhood and previous relationships. As I unraveled my past and the defense mechanism (a.k.a. masks), I learned the abyss went deeper than I thought. It was like an onion being unwrapped one layer at a time.

Codependency ran my entire life. What did that mean? As a child, when there was chaos in my youth, I learned to just go along with whatever was happening to keep the peace for the person imposing the pressure and abuse. I was programmed to play different roles to keep the balance in my chaotic home.

I learned to not say anything when the boy in kindergarten class used to put his hand down my pants in reading class. The teachers never saw it. I learned to suppress my needs and became invisible, and this cycle continued throughout my life with boys and men. I learned to hide my true identity through submission, sweetness, and obedience.

In my younger years, I played the roles of the good girl, the godly woman, and the hero. I grew into a mistress, seductress, addict, and rebel as life got bitter. I flipped between Angel and Devil personas, as it went well with the strict religious programming I learned in my upbringing.

I allowed those personas to come out and play, and I accepted them as the parts that tried to protect me and survive in an environment and culture that didn't sustain humanity's well-being.

Peeling the onions made me cry, but I continued peeling more layers away. As I peeled, deeper traumas and patterns went beyond my own life. I explored the ways of my religious upbringing, the environment I lived in, the people I knew, and the society I was programmed in. That our parents were programmed in; where does this trauma come from, and why are these patterns here?

5th Episode: Embracing the Truth

I dove deeper into the abyss and learned more about racism, the genocide of the indigenous peoples, patriarchy, white supremacy, ancestry, the history of humankind, and the inter-generational and social trauma that has shaped our culture and society. And therefore, I started to take off the masks that societal programming trained me into.

The masks I learned to wear as a woman in our society were to reach specific expectations and standards that I could not reach; the expectations of how I should look, dress, weigh, act, obey and submit to the patriarchy of our times.

I was unruly, bold, independent, and loud when I was younger. As a teen, I moved from a substantially diverse city on the west coast to a small white Christian town in mid-central IL. Let's say I didn't fit in as a gangster who wore baggy clothes and wanted to be a rapper called Crazzy with two z's.

When I moved, I got many threats and was bullied severely. I learned that who I am was wrong and would not be tolerated; therefore, it was safer to convert to Christianity at the age of thirteen.

I felt pushed into submission to be able to survive my teenage years. I changed into the good religious girl that followed all the rules, worked hard, pleased everyone, got a conservative higher education, and married a Pastor.

I left the church and my husband when I was 26 years old after being accused and put on display for saying something "out of line." I was told to step down from my ministry duties and to honor and obey my husband, who was abusive to me.

Even though I left the faith years ago, the training and programming were a part of my behavior and belief system for another decade. I slowly healed the angsty inner teen within me and had to release myself from these standards.

In the Fall of 2021, I was diagnosed with ADHD. I struggled with other neuro-divergent mental diagnoses throughout my life, but this one changed me completely. I was able to take off the mask of perfectionism and masking. It had been hard to accept my divergent nature throughout my entire life. I always felt self-conscious and out of place. I repressed how different and weird I felt inside and have struggled to come to terms with it.

Finale Episode: Death to Rebirth

Radical self-acceptance has been a lifelong journey for me. When I pretended to be just like everyone else, I felt very alone and alienated. I tried to keep to the status quo but was unhappy and depressed. As I took these masks off, I realized how natural it was for me to live exciting experiences and a unique proactive life; to live uninhibited and vibrantly.

I began to realize that I wanted to have the capacity for unconditional self-love, embrace an optimistic, joyous expression of myself, and be an agent of change for others by pushing them outside of their comfort zones so they can take off their masks.

The person I saw in the mirror may have seemed worn down, tired, or out of their mind, especially from wearing all those masks for 38 years; but after doing the work to take them off, it was time to be more of my unique, authentic self.

Who would that be? It might be an adventure to see. The masks have been taken off, and now it's time to be free. I hope others will feel inspired and encouraged to do the same. Loving yourself unconditionally is not selfish – it is our right and our life's intention. The greatest rebellious act you can ever play.

About the Author:
Tiffany McBride

Tiffany McBride (She, Her, They, Them) is an LCPC, Reiki Master Teacher, Shaman, Author, and Expressive Artist. They run their own practice, Holistic Vibrations, LLC., in Bloomington IL.

Tiffany began writing song lyrics, poetry, and short stories as a young girl. They have continued to utilize writing into their academia, their hobbies, and coping skills throughout their life. Tiffany became a published author at the age of 38 and plans to continue to write more books into the future.

Tiffany enjoys reading self-help, psychology, history, and spiritual literature. Tiffany has achieved many certificates and trainings and is currently working on their Doctorate in Shamanic Psycho-Spiritual Studies.

In Tiffany's downtime, they also love to blog, paint, draw, play the ukulele and guitar, sing, be in nature, kayak, camp, hammock, take photographs, go to concerts, and hang with friends.

Connect with them on the following sites:
Website: https://www.tiffany-mcbride.org/
Facebook Group for Women/Non-Binary:
SHEE: ReWilding The Sacred Yoni
//www.facebook.com/groups/1057289361484274
Instagram://www.instagram.com/witchycrowwmn83/
Blog: https://www.tiffany-mcbride.org/blog

Who am I, really?

Chapter 5

Not even a pandemic:
One working mom's struggle

by Regina DuRocher Keefe

From the day they were born, I wanted to be at home with them. Often the only working mom among my mom groups, I had to leave my girls at home while the others were able to stay home with their kids. It was the supportive kind of mom groups where we compared parenting tips and stories. We helped each other through the hard stuff, celebrated the good stuff, and vented about everything in between.

The side effect of being the only working mom in the group is it highlighted what I was missing out on. Not on purpose, but this was my life and that was their life. I wanted that life.

The kind where you have time to do the DIY art projects, read every page of every book on their overflowing bookshelves, and take day trips that end in a camera roll full of sweet, smiling, round cheeks and tired kids who fall asleep before you make it out of the parking lot.

The kind where you actually do all the things that I keep telling my kids we will do soon. That's what I wished I could have. Instead the list of all the things 'we want to do sometime' kept growing, as I kept mentally searching for the next weekend we wouldn't be busy.

Over the years some of my mom friends went back to work as the kids got older, but when you've been a working mom from the beginning, there's just always something that separates you. I made peace with the fact that, no matter how much I wanted it, that life was not in the cards for me. COVID made me realize I hadn't really made peace with it at all.

Laughter filled the table, chips and queso being shared, dollar margaritas, Mexican music filling the air around us as we unwound at a mom's night out. It was January. I remember the air was cold and crisp when I got out of the car and quickly made my way to the door. The smell of spices warmed me as I inhaled, and the sound of sizzling plates competed with the rumbling of my stomach.

We were excited to be out of the house, kids left at home and, hopefully, in bed. We hadn't done a mom's night over the holiday months because schedules had been so hectic.

You could hear chatter throughout the room, plates clinking and laughter from our table as we shared our stories and our salsa. Someone mentioned the new virus, I guess we had all heard about it, but I wasn't even sure what the virus was at that point.

I said what I always say when parents bring up viruses, "I'll do my best not to lick any door knobs."

I've never stressed much over a virus. I stress about a lot of other things that don't make much sense, but catching viruses wasn't one of them. I figured exposure builds immunity, and we are a working, active family so we are just out in it. We can't just stay home because it is the cold and flu season.

We would do the same as we always do, wash our hands, avoid people if they're sick and my other favorite "cold" joke, "Don't let anyone cough into your mouth." Looking back, I feel a little apologetic for brushing it off. I couldn't have known how much things would change.

Concern slowly crept in. March 2, 2020, I was more careful than normal when I flew to Baltimore for a work trip. I didn't use the hand rails. I didn't touch anything I wasn't buying at the gift shop. Too many people from too many places touching all the same things took on a new meaning.

The trip was filled with seminars and business dinners. I didn't think much about the virus the rest of the week. I enjoyed the quiet time to read, talking to the girls and my husband, Scott at night. Cora, our 6 year old, asked how many days until I got back, Lydia, our 11 year old, gave me the recap of everything happening at home and in her fifth grade classroom.

By the end of the week I was ready to get home. I valued having peace and quiet, but I missed the chaos after a few lonely nights in a hotel. A coworker and I were lucky enough to catch a ride back to the airport with some colleagues. On the 45 minute drive, my usual anxiety over city traffic was non-existent.

It was replaced by dread. Instead of gripping the door handle until my knuckles were white, I tried to breathe in slowly as if that would somehow make us share less air. The woman in the front seat of the car had been sick all week long and hadn't left her room. She had skipped every seminar.

Now I was too close, breathing her germ-filled, recycled air in this compact rental car for 45 minutes in rush hour traffic leaving Baltimore. This was the first time I remember being concerned about catching a virus. It would not be the last.

March 9, 2020. My concern was growing. I still wasn't scared. It all seemed far away—some imaginary phantom people talk about as if they've seen it, but never really have. I live in Central Illinois, in a relatively rural town of around 20,000 people. The first case in our county wouldn't be reported until March 24th.

COVID hadn't yet hit our community. There was talk about a lock down. We would have to stay home for two weeks. People said we should get supplies. What would that even look like?

In my head, it meant people staying home. Empty streets, shuttered businesses—like a movie scene. The unknown was unsettling. I was less concerned about the actual virus than about those unknowns. Will we have enough food and supplies? Will my parents have enough at home? What will people do?

The shelves became barer every day. The week before the shutdown was our normal grocery run, so we went to the store and got our supplies and made the same jokes everyone else did about panicking and buying too much.

THE CHAOS OF COVID

We felt better laughing at the sight of empty bread shelves because anything else was scary. On March 13th it was official. The White House had announced that there would be a shut down.

Despite the growing concern in the pit of my stomach, sandwiched in between jokes to make us feel better, I felt a bit of hope and dare I say excitement. I could stay home with my kids for 2 weeks! I remember when the girls had their tonsils taken out on the same day. We scheduled them together because I didn't have enough time off to do them separately.

The two weeks home with my girls after their same-day surgery were the best weeks of my life. Memories were made. Picnic lunches of applesauce and ice cream as we laid under the tree on blankets, pointing out bunnies and pirate ships in the clouds.

We could have that again! My kids would be out of school and although I had sick time to cover it, I believed my employer would give us permission to work from home. I was lucky to have paid time off and felt horrible for other working parents who didn't. Even so, I allowed myself some joy with this excuse to stay home with my kids.

Work scrambled. Who had computers at home? How could we work from home during a shutdown? My laptop was old, but it would have to do. The girls came home from school with Chromebooks. We didn't even have the internet at the time—I know, weird, for 2020 but we just used our phones.

I found a provider who quickly set up our wi-fi. We were ready. I daydreamed about helping the girls do reading and math, art projects we hoped to try, board games, laughter, and snuggles. The girls were in 5th grade and Kindergarten. 11 and 6 years old. I was going to take advantage of every moment I had with them.

Except, I didn't get to. Friday, March 13th came and went, and work never announced that we would shut down. My parents took turns watching the girls and helping them with school work. My job was deemed essential because I work in finance. My husband's job was deemed essential because he is a delivery driver for a major shipping service.

Life changed for so many people that day, that month, that year.

But everyday life didn't change for us, not in the ways I expected it to. My kids' lives changed. Cora's first year of school was cut short, Lydia's last year at elementary school was ripped out from under her. They couldn't see their friends except on Zoom calls. My parents' lives changed. They were now my kids' teachers and caregivers.

Nothing changed for me except my growing emotions. The guilt didn't change, I had to leave them every day, despite them begging me to stay home. It was gut-wrenching to hear Cora cry that I was leaving her. It broke my heart to see Lydia disappointed I couldn't stay home but also try to be mature like she wasn't upset.

I came home exhausted, as did my husband—too worn out to do the things we wanted. We didn't have a choice. We had to work. The girls had to stay home and do remote learning. Cora was having trouble—kindergarten is not meant to be finished alone.

I tried everything possible. I tried multiple methods but still couldn't keep her motivated. Lydia adjusted much easier. She wasn't happy but she had a phone and ways to talk to them still, so she didn't feel as cut off.

No, life didn't change for us the way I expected it to, and that's when I got angry. For years I had tucked a small amount of hope inside of me, but now, deep in the pit of my stomach, I could feel anger devouring it. The void feeling of an empty stomach was all I had left. Look, I knew I would never be a stay at home mom. I clung to the idea that I could still find a way to do the special things, make all the special memories and go to work.

I clung to the idea that I could balance it all. I clung to the idea that it was ok that I had to go to work, and that I didn't have to feel guilty about it. But this...this pandemic...it brought it all up to the surface. Like when you feel the vomit in your mouth, but you swallow it just in time. So that's what I did. I swallowed it.

Not even a pandemic was enough for me to stay home with my kids. And then the guilt grew. If I complained about going to work, people would respond, "At least you have a job."

They were right, and I was thankful to provide for my family, but that didn't make the other feelings any easier. I still wanted to be home with my kids. I wanted to keep my family safe.

I could not do either of those things. I worried my family would get COVID. I worried more about spreading it. My husband delivered well over 100 stops a day. What if one of us got it, gave it to him, and then he touched all those packages? I feared he could spread the virus to 100 people in a single day.

Every person visiting my office made my anxiety worse. By 2020, I was at my job for 15 years. I'm in the business of serving people and I've always been happy to help but every time someone's hand reached for our door handle, my stomach dropped like I was on a roller coaster.

I felt the panic creep into my chest and burn my throat as I tried to swallow the worry away. That feeling expanded over time. At first it lasted a moment; I would take back control, but as time went on, it became harder and harder for me to be in charge of my responses. I knew it was a problem; I'm thankful I was aware of my anxiety, but I felt helpless to change it. I had no choice but to go to work, to help customers, and to do my best to not catch COVID-19.

My Type 1 Diabetes put me at risk. I have been diabetic since I was 12. My immune system is compromised because of it, along with having a second autoimmune disease, Hashimoto's Thyroiditis. While some people kept responding to the threat of COVID-19 by acting like it was nothing more than the flu, I had to be careful.

I wasn't sure how my body would be affected if I caught the virus. When our household gets a stomach bug I take longer to get over it and I'm sicker because my immune system is weaker. I have never had Influenza before, but the claim that COVID-19 is *just like the flu* is dismissive to anyone with a compromised immune system. It would knock us out of commission for a long time, or worse, forever. I had a conversation with my husband after I felt we had been careless and put ourselves at risk.

Nothing done was intentional, but I realized he didn't have the same thoughts cross his mind as I did. I asked him what he would tell the girls if they got COVID, if I got COVID, and I died. Of course he didn't have an answer because he hadn't considered that as a real possibility. I reminded him they were kids. I had no doubt that if they believed they gave me the Virus, and I got sick and died, they would have this thought for the rest of their lives, "I killed my mom."

We could not risk this. I couldn't jeopardize my kids that way.

To complicate things we listed and sold our home of 13 years just three weeks into the shut-down. We couldn't believe it had sold so quickly, but we were thankful. After every house showing, I wiped down every knob, every light switch, every countertop, every door handle in the house. If there was a chance some stranger had touched it, I wiped it down.

Moving to our new home gave us something to look forward to. The excitement almost made life feel normal again. When the weather was nice we were able to take calculated risks as we called them, and see people outside. The girls rejoiced at being able to see their friends again. I had pangs of guilt after every gathering because I felt like such a hypocrite. I needed to see my kids happy again.

They needed to be included in gatherings. All my mom friends were at home with their kids and were involved in these small groups with the same handful of friends to limit the risk. We weren't always able to be a part of that. We couldn't offer to watch other people's kids, because we weren't home. Would other parents even want us to be a part of their little circle?

We were still exposed every day at work to potential risks. I think I realized at this point that most of my concerns were those I was projecting outward onto the situation. They added another difficult level to what was a difficult time already. So we did the best we could.

We were lucky. We made it all the way to December 2020 before any of us had a close call. I got the phone call from the middle school nurse while I was at work. Lydia was exposed to someone at school that had tested positive for COVID-19. She was going to be in quarantine. My heart sank. Part of me tried to be calm; we knew it was almost inevitable that it would happen to our family, but part of me hoped if we did all the right things, we could just avoid it.

Part of me wanted to panic while frantically thinking about what we were going to do, what changes we would have to make for the next two weeks, but there wasn't time to panic. The nurse explained that the exposure had happened on Thursday, the 3rd. We didn't get the call until the 7th! The office didn't know that the other student tested positive until Friday and by the time the school and health department could call to notify people, it was Monday.

Four days had already passed. I wasn't just devastated that she was exposed and could potentially get it, but I was even more destroyed at the idea that we could have exposed my parents and some of our friends over the weekend. To make matters worse, we had celebrated Cora's 7th birthday that Saturday. I had to call the parents of the other children who had taken the chance at sending their kids to our house and break the news to them.

It took a while to make each call. I had to get up the nerve before hitting that little green phone each and every time, but I knew I had to do it. I could confidently tell them that she had no symptoms, and she wears her mask at school every day so the chances were as minimal as they could be. Everyone took the news well. I was grateful for the grace they gifted me. It did nothing to ease my guilt.

We made a plan. The new house had a good setup for quarantine. Lydia could stay in her room, which had a bathroom attached to it. Cora could use the bathroom downstairs, and we would be able to stay apart. We purchased a mini fridge with a microwave on top and put it in Lydia's room. We bought her groceries to keep in her room, condiments, easy things to heat up, drinks, and snacks.

Anything that had to be cooked downstairs in the kitchen, we made and took up to her. The first couple days we felt ok. I would sit on the top of the steps on one side of the hallway, my back up against the closet door. Lydia sat in the doorway of her room. We wore our masks. We laughed. We talked. But we didn't hug…we didn't get too close.

At first we staved off the tears, but it got harder as the days went by. The emotional rollercoaster we were on would have put any spectacular Disney ride to shame. First, there was excitement. Lydia had her own little apartment. She was thrilled to have a mini fridge, snacks all to herself, and she didn't have to go to school. And the time clock wasn't just two weeks, it was almost an entire month. Her two week quarantine took her to the 18th, the last Friday before Winter break started. The district didn't return to school until Jan 4, 2021. She was out for the rest of the calendar year. To a 6th grader, this seemed awesome, like every junior high student's dream come true. However, boredom set in after a few days. We laughed a lot when she said she wanted to come out of her room.

Before her quarantine we were lucky if she ever wanted to hang out with us, spending most of her time up in her room by choice. But tell an almost teenager that they have to stay in her room and suddenly she doesn't want to be there anymore and misses you. Despair was the 2nd stage of emotions.

Then there was anger. Lydia found out that the boy who had exposed her, got to go back to school.

"Why does he get to go back to school, and I don't?"

I talked her through the technical side of things: the math of how the CDC and health department counted the days from when someone tests positive and how his clock started well before her exposure, but no one knew. She didn't care about the science of it all. It wasn't fair. That's the only part that she felt.

He was the one who didn't wear his mask right; he was the one who was corrected all day long to pull up his mask; he was the one who exposed her. He left school the day before she did, but he got to return to school a week before her. It felt unfair to her. There is no amount of parenting that takes away the sting a child feels when life is unfair. All I could say was I was sorry. But then…it got so much worse.

On December 11th, 2020, my Dad called me with the heartbreaking news that my Uncle Bob had passed away. He died from COVID-19. I was in disbelief. Just a few days earlier the doctors had mentioned improvement, and said he was responding to some of the treatments.

Despite being on the ventilator, I thought he was going to get better. Now I was being told he was just…gone. It all happened so fast. He had gotten the virus, and soon after they had to call the ambulance because he had difficulty breathing. Within days he was on the ventilator.

Should I have been more prepared for the news? I'm not sure. It just felt impossible. He got it, but he would be fine. He had to be fine. Until he wasn't. Now I had the job of telling my daughters he was dead. My children are no strangers to death and funerals; nothing could have prepared them for this loss, however.

How do you tell one of your daughters that her uncle is dead, from the same virus she has been exposed to, but don't worry honey, you'll be fine. This was the first time I had hugged my daughter in a week. Virus be damned. Risk thrown out the window. My daughter needed me and the only comfort I could give her was holding her against me as she cried.

Kids are often so unafraid, seemingly invincible in their own minds. They think, 'that will never happen to me'. That confidence left Lydia like a car going 0-60. There was nothing I could do to take her fear away. We had just come over the next hill of the rollercoaster, about to plummet down to the unknown. I thought that was the hardest conversation I would have about Uncle Bob.

I was wrong again.

I didn't tell Cora for two days. I couldn't bring myself to do it. Cora had a special bond with Bob. They didn't get to see each other that often, but when they did there was just something special about their interactions. I wasn't ready to tell her, but someone expressed their sympathy to me in front of her that caused her to ask, "Wait, Bob who? My best friend, Bob."

I saw her heart break when I told her. The tears soaked through my shirt as I held her on my lap. "I'm so sorry," was all I could say to her. The panic I saw flash across her eyes was excruciating when I saw her make the connection that he died of COVID, and that Lydia was in quarantine for COVID.

For months to follow, Cora slept with this giant stuffed black lab dog, a gift from Uncle Bob. She cried about how she didn't get a chance to tell him goodbye. She woke up some mornings and out of the blue asked me if I knew who her best friend forever was? To then declare, Bob.

"He was my best friend. He really liked hanging out with me. And sometimes while he was eating he would watch me golf. He liked that. He was my best buddy."

I can honestly say that she has never gotten over losing him. A year and a half later, she remains crushed that she did not get to say goodbye.

Lydia was out of quarantine on the 18th. We prepared to celebrate the holiday. We had the most beautiful real tree, a first for us. 10 feet tall, to fit in our new living room with a vaulted ceiling. We argued the entire time we tried to get it inside the house and into the tree stand, but she was a beauty.

Scott was a real Clark Griswold that year. It felt good to celebrate. Lydia never did come down with COVID, to our relief. We didn't get to properly say goodbye to Bob because we couldn't have a funeral. We couldn't celebrate how we normally would. However, it was a truly memorable Christmas. There is so often stress clouding an otherwise bright and enjoyable day and staying home eliminated so much of it. It felt good to be happy and forget about all the struggles we had been facing for one day.

Winter break ended and both the kids returned to school. Cora came down with a stomach bug and missed about a week of school. We tested for COVID, but she was negative. I sent her back to school just long enough for her to be exposed to a kid who had tested positive for the virus.

We were back to quarantine. We moved the mini fridge from Lydia's room to hers, which she was very excited about. She was excited not to go school too. The excitement wore off the same way a kid grows tired of a new toy they begged for but then never touches again once you open the package. It was so much harder for Cora to be in quarantine.

I stayed home from work the first week with her. This made Lydia incredibly mad at me, because I had not stayed home with her like I did her sister. Her anger made my already existing guilt spread like wildfire. It was also more difficult to stay away from a 7 year old. I caved like any mother would have after a couple days of whining.

Our living room happens to have a 1970's sunken living room attached to it, so we decided Cora could hang out there, so she could still be with us. We designated the rocking chair as her chair. We still made her wear her mask. Lydia made sure to express her displeasure with us at every opportunity. I didn't blame her. I tried to make her understand for my own sake. I didn't want to feel more like a failure as a mother than I already did.

When I told someone how much we were struggling, how hard it had been to keep them in their rooms and stay apart from them, I became furious. Not because of my own struggle. Because the response was to tell me that when their relative was in quarantine they did nothing different other than keep them home from school.

They didn't stay apart, they didn't wear masks, they changed nothing. We did everything we were supposed to do and taking it seriously. It was causing us grief and heartache. It was so disheartening to hear others weren't.

Was I putting my children through this for nothing? My uncle was dead. I wasn't sure how my body would handle it if I got the virus. It didn't feel like I was overreacting. It felt like I was doing the right thing. Why as a parent, is the right thing often so hard?

As a parent, all I want to do is not screw up my kids too much. I know some of it is inevitable. We have done our best. We make the best choices that we can with the information we have at the time. I question myself every step of the way. There will never be a clear way, or definite answers.

I won't pretend there was one simple way to navigate through the pandemic. I saw so many parents on one side, and so many on the other. I know the struggle was hard for us all, no matter which side we stood on. For our family, it was crushing at times. The weight of trying to make the right choice, the guilt that came with second guessing everything we did were at times too much to bear.

I was thankful for those other moms in my support group. We may not have been living the exact same lives, we may not have been faced with the same exact struggles, but we all struggled, nonetheless. I am certain I made mistakes; before, and during the pandemic. I have always wanted my life with the girls to be different. I kept this little dream tucked away, knowing it would never happen but for some reason clinging to it.

Then COVID came and it ruined so many things. It stole so much from us. It churned up so many feelings I tried to keep down for so long. I guess I can't be mad at the end of the day that my employer wanted me to come to work and do my job.

I am just mad that my safety, the safety of my family, the safety of those around me, just wasn't enough.

Not even a pandemic could give me the chance to stay home with my girls. Not even a pandemic was enough to put safety over making money. Not even a pandemic was enough to give me the chance to do something right and keep my kids safe. Not even a pandemic was enough to bring our community and our country together to protect each other. Not even a pandemic was enough.

Not even a pandemic....

About the Author
Regina DuRocher Keefe

Regina DuRocher Keefe is an aspiring author, making her debut in this collaboration. Her education has revolved around art, with focuses in art history and ceramics. She surprisingly finds herself with a career in finance, having 17 years of experience.

Recently, she began to explore her spiritual side in a way that deepens her connection with those around her and allows her to express her gifts with the world. As one door seemingly opens another; she looks forward to what may come.

Regina is forever grateful for the love and support from her husband, Scott of 18 years, who thinks she is a witch but doesn't really know what that means. They share two spirited daughters; Lydia, 13, and Cora, 8. Someday she will be grateful for their sense of adventure, attitude and independence. For today, those characteristics make her an exhausted mother.

Balancing marriage, motherhood, work, and her own interests is Regina's greatest challenge. However, she believes everything happens for a reason, exactly when it needs to, so she continues to trust the journey.

A fierce supporter of friends, she can often be found in groups of women encouraging others to be their authentic selves. She has led baby-wearing and breastfeeding groups in Central Illinois where she made lifelong friendships.

THE CHAOS OF COVID

Regina thinks everyone could benefit from therapy. She believes having uncomfortable conversations is important. The mother of two pit-bulls, she encourages everyone to look past stereotypes and adopt a rescue. She thinks adding cello to any song makes it better, powerful works of art should spark emotion, and she believes in Santa. If you can't prove to her it doesn't exist, then she will always believe it's possible.

Not even a pandemic.

Chapter 6

The Long Road Home:
Confusion, Panic & The Sanity of NPR

By Dr. Ruth A. Souther

I woke up in a panic, my curly, red hair sticky with sweat, with a thin glaze covering my pale face. My heart was pounding and confusion blurring my vision. For a few seconds, I didn't remember where I was. I threw off the blankets and sat up only to meet the concerned gaze of my friend Terri.

"What was that about? Were you having a nightmare?" Terri was sitting on her bed in the hotel room reading emails, blonde hair in a messy bun with curling tendrils on her smooth forehead.

"Yes, it was a crazy dream." I rubbed my face with both hands and quieted my breath. "I dreamed I couldn't get home. Everything was closed. All the gas stations were out of fuel, and restaurants, even fast food joints, had no food to offer. Even worse, the state borders were all shut down. I couldn't get home!"

Panic started to rise again, and believe me, I am not the sort to panic but the events that unfolded in my sleep were just too real.

"I couldn't get out of Texas and back to Illinois. Everything was shut down, airports, grocery stores—people were fighting for supplies. It was like the apocalypse."

"Or a Zombie invasion? That's what it sounds like to me–a Zombie apocalypse! We are in a good place for it, though, up here in the hotel where they would have trouble getting to us." Terri pursed her lips in a thoughtful expression. "We don't have any weapons. Is there a vendor downstairs that has swords?"

"Probably," I laughed. Terri always makes me feel better.

I was so excited to go to Dallas-Ft. Worth-Arlington—my first trip to Texas since my friend Terri moved there eight years ago. Ridiculous that it had been so long, but time just moves fast these days and before I knew it, here we were.

Terri and I talked for hours to plan our vending booth, how it would be arranged, and which books to display. We both are board members of Crystal Heart Imprints, (CHI) a collaborative publishing company with many books to CHI's credit. We also knew that every book had its own niche and audience, and not all were suited for this kind of convention.

We made careful choices because of the small area assigned to us in the vendors' room. Since both of us were chosen to give workshops, one of us had to be present at our booth at all times. There's a lot that goes into how to display our merchandise and have the right signage to draw people over.

We know we have charming, chatty personalities, however that is not always enough. The booth must be attractive, too. So, hours and hours of preparation.

I was a bit nervous about driving into the metro area in the evening rush hours, therefore, I decided to spend the night in Arkansas. I wanted to be fresh and alert when I hit all that traffic. Not to mention, I'm in my sixties and driving wears me out.

The thrill of the adventure could've kept me going but I knew it was best that I rested because we would launch right into setting up our booth as soon as I got there Thursday afternoon. The event was a sci-fi/fantasy/witchy kind of convention to promote not only our books, and merchandise but also a festival we created that would happen in Springfield, IL

Naked Magik, due to happen June 2020, right on the Summer Solstice. We had a lot riding on the festivals we were scheduled to attend that spring. We planned to promote, promote, promote Naked Magik as we had a lot of money invested in it. We invited our favorite musician/singers from Poland, Laboratorium Piesni (Song Laboratory) and although they are worth it, it was an expensive endeavor.

We hoped to draw people from across the country to celebrate the holistic nature of Springfield, IL. It is a truly phenomenal community who supports each other rather than the backbiting and jealousy we had experienced at other events. We've even been told that Springfield is a vortex of healing and inspiration, and we both deeply believe this is true.

When we put out the call to local facilitators, we had great response and now we were in the marketing and advertising mode. Not to mention, our intention to have as much fun as possible since we had not seen each other for a long while.

We dragged in heavy boxes and tubs filled with our merchandise, as well as tablecloths, signage, and sundry other items. We had a special notebooks ready for participants to sign our Naked Magik email list, business cards and advertisement. We even had a sound system for some of the workshops. Remember that the next time you're walking through an event and see all the pretty displays—it's helluva lot of planning and work.

Our booth with custom-designed t-shirts that announced 'Witched Good Vibes' in support of Terri's Black Cauldron, a cozy mystery paranormal series, which were also displayed on the table, along with her handcrafted and unique mystic pens and burn books. The idea behind the pens and the books was to write your deepest, darkest thoughts. Or your highest desire to achieve, or your wild, raw magical self that communes with the Fairies. And then, much to the horror of those buying the set, burn or bury the book and pen at the end of a year and a day.

Most argued that the books and pens were simply too gorgeous to do such a thing to them, and yet in the end, Terri always convinced the buyer this was the greatest gift they could give themselves. The entire purpose was to release all those emotions, judgments, beliefs and aspirations to the Universe to be carried out in the greater scheme of the cosmos.

Also on our table was my Tarot workbook—years of teaching classes compiled into one source, The Elemental Priestess workbook, Tarot cards, handmade witchy beaded bracelets, and my novels based on Greek mythology. Those stories explored the gods and goddess of old and the hidden truths that went untold in classic mythology. I'm proud of being a channel for these ancient ones to tell the actual happenings rather than the victimization of the feminine and the stance of all the males were brutally seeking pleasure or pain no matter what the cost.

During the setup, we got to know some of the other vendors, even exchanged phone numbers and emails. The room was fairly vibrating with anticipation and filled with laughter, talk and the clatter of setting up booths. Some early shopping was allowed, and we were thrilled to already be in the thick of sales. This was going to be a profitable and connected event—we were certain of it.

You could just feel the buoyancy in the vendor room.

I was the first to have a workshop presentation on Tarot—one of my favorite subjects. I've studied Tarot for thirty years and I'm very good at it, to say the least. Knowledge, humor, plus my experience, and we were off and running. The workshop was well attended, and again, illustrated the positive sense of how this event would financially support our efforts as well as the promotion of Naked Magik. Terri even made a meme of me while I was teaching—my very first one.

We were riding high!

After the vendor room closed, we adjourned to a small restaurant/bar in the hotel to meet a friend of Terri's. She has long wanted us to come across each other, and it was finally happening. Yet another delightful happenstance.

Other vendors were also gathered there, as well as some presenters and organizers. We had a few drinks, ate dinner, and laughed our asses off getting to know each other. When we finally headed to our room, we were exhausted, happy, and anticipating the next day when the vendors got to shop each other's wares before the doors opened to the public.

When the nightmare woke me in the morning, it made no sense. After the fun of the evening before, where did that come from? No idea, until....

"Wait. What?" I stared at Terri as she again read a text from one of the vendors.

"Hurry and come down to the vender's room. We have until 11 am to shop each other's merchandise before the hotel closes at noon."

"What?" I repeated. "But why?"

"I don't know," Terri responded. "This is weird."

"Really weird," I repeated. Flashes of my nightmare popped into my mind as we rushed to get dressed.

Once we ran down to the lobby of the hotel, we found confusion as other vendors ran back and forth in the corridors. Some were already hauling their stuff out in wagons and rolling racks. The line to the service desk was long, and loud voices were heard protesting the change in plans.

Terri and I looked at each other in shock, still not understanding what was happening. We rushed to the vendor's room, down a long open galley where displays were already pulled apart and loaded into wagons and carts. And then along another corridor where there was more shouting, swearing, and uncertainty.

Inside the large room was pure chaos.

The evening before the venue had been a thing of beauty with colorful tables and displays, some with art, some with detailed little replicas of comic book characters and superheroes, many with crafted items like jewelry, cloaks, hats, and costuming. There were drums in one corner and gorgeous, hand carved flutes in another. Across the room were proud authors and artists who displayed the culmination of their hard work, some for the first time. The plethora of shopping possibilities was intriguing, and we were so looking forward to having the time to explore.

Even though the text said we could still shop this morning, by the time we arrived, that was no longer an option.

The convention was cancelled. All guests were being ushered out. The hotel had been ordered to close. There was an outbreak of the corona virus in Dallas and a city-wide shut down of all public buildings had been issued.

March 2020. COVID-19 had arrived.

We packed up everything as fast as we could and loaded our wagons to take out to the car. Every move was mirrored by others frantic to leave before they forced us out. There was palpable fear that the hotel would send security to clear the room and force us to leave our belongings behind. Everyone had a lot of money invested in their wares, and to be suddenly locked out of the room was a terrifying thought.

As we were fighting the panicked crowd to get through to the parking area, a storm rolled in. Thunder crashed and boomed, shaking the building as lightening forked across a dark sky. Rain came down in torrents, flooding the streets in short order. Terri had parked in the hotel's garage—I had parked in the outer edge without cover. I was drenched by the time I loaded up all the boxes of books and tubs of miscellaneous items, like the sound system, whiteboard, and easel.

We hadn't even packed our clothes yet. Not just everyday clothing but also costumes, jewelry, makeup, and hair products. Being at one of these events means you did your best to stand out, one way or the other, Terri and I always chose creative costuming, many of which are bulky and heavy, borrowed from our belly dance years. What can I say, they were too pretty and expensive to just donate, so we repurposed them into festival/convention wearables.

Terri wanted me to wait until the rain slowed, and said we could get lunch first, but the weather channel showed a huge line of thunderstorms all across the area I had to drive so it wouldn't make a difference when I left.

And there was that frightening dream. Yet here we were in the physical world facing those exact circumstances—businesses closing their doors under government orders—the idea that there would be no gas, no food and state borders blocked to stop the spread of this virus seemed like a real possibility.

As I said before, I'm not prone to panic or anxiety but both were in full bloom at that point. I felt I had to go. Now.

Right now.

We said our goodbyes and good lucks and I headed out. Thankfully, I had a full tank of gas and snacks left over from the drive down. I felt a bit better knowing I didn't need to stop for a long while as I left Dallas-Fort

Worth and headed to the Arkansas state line. I was worried there would be State Police barricading the road, turning people back like they do when there's a blizzard.

The first thing I did was turn on NPR, a news source I trust. I listened to Dr. Fauci try to calm the masses in his dry voice. I heard the interviewer asking all the right questions, the ones I needed answers to as well.

Except there were no concrete responses. It was all a dark mass of confusion, fear and worse, reports of presidential denial that anything was happening. We had a president who refused to believe it was real and promoted the exact opposite of what would help contain the infections. Dr. Fauci did his best to explain what he could but was helpless in the face of the highest level of contradiction.

Many states' governors were ordering shutdowns with the intention of keeping their constituents safe on the advisement of the CDC and President of the United States. Other governors were arguing there was no need to go to those extremes.

My mind went into a whirlwind of what ifs. On a regular day, I love to play the What If game. In fact, in many of my classes, the What If game has become a staple, but in a positive way. An example: what if you could live your life with an empowered presence?

What if you broke away from those negative people in your life and created a new pattern of happiness? What if you wrote that novel, moved to a different state, or got a different job? There is no limit to how the game can pan out and often ends up with laughter and an uplifted view for those who are involved in the class.

This time, though, it was not a fun thing. The What If

game was terrifying.

What if there were no groceries, or gas? What would businesses do if they were shut down? How would the workers survive? How would restaurants and other service-oriented industries manage? How about all the office workers? And schools?

Another horrible What If. What if my husband or one of our children, grandchildren or great-grandchildren developed Covid? What if close friends, or elderly family/friends came down with this killing machine? I could not even contemplate that and forced my thoughts back to the bigger picture.

How would churches, gyms, grocery stores, warehouses, big box and small commerce, line production, and manufacturing plants all handle this unforeseen, unbelievable turn of events?

On and on and on, my mind scrambled to make sense of this. At the time I was sixty-seven and had never in my life seen such an apocalyptic-feeling moment. It was like all the disaster movies rolled into one but happening in real time.

I was in 6th grade when President Kennedy was assassinated, turning the United States on its ear, I was in high school when Dr. Martin Luther King Jr. was assassinated, and racial justice rose into my small-town mentality as I began to understand bigger issues.

The Vietnam War was a weird, scary time with the draft, as I had and a brother, a boyfriend, and many other friends old enough to go fight. I saw the hippie movement, the rejection of those old values of war, money and regular jobs, and an embracing of free love and drugs.

I remember wanting to be a flower child, a

quintessential hippie, if you will. I did my best in Broadlands, Illinois to be counterculture, and thankfully, I had parents who weren't too bothered by my rebellion.

When the twin towers fell in 2001, I was at work. We all stared in disbelief as this disaster created by terrorists unfolded in front of us. We came together as a nation in an emotional crisis, caring more for our fellow humans in a way I had never witnessed.

All this and so much more was a wild storm of random strings tied in from the past as the future lie in uncertainty. So much upheaval, so much panic and horror, but we as a nation, as the United States of America, always came together and moved through the series of tragedies. I hoped we could do the same with this pandemic.

Pandemic. A word that I had not heard used in modern times. Pandemics were back in the time of bubonic plagues and scarlet fever—when hundreds of thousands of people died horrible deaths. That simply could not be what was happening now, in 2020, right?

Unfortunately, yes. Yes it could and did. The numbers of dead and infected rose and rose, and still there were those who continued to deny Covid was real.

"It is nothing but the regular flu. This hysteria is ridiculous."

There were those people who would not (or perhaps to be kind, could not) get the vaccination when it finally came out. My husband and I got our vaccination as fast as we could.

But I digress.

The message was to wear masks (I didn't have any), and gloves, or use hand sanitizer after touching anything. I didn't have that either. I had to stop in Arkansas to get gas, go to the bathroom and get food. I did have some baby wipes in my car and used that to clean the pump handle and pulled my sleeve over my fingers to open doors, as well as being careful to wash my hands every chance I had.

No one seemed concerned in Arkansas. Business as usual. It was the strangest thing, watching these people move around as if there was not a single thing wrong in the world. Or maybe they also thought it was too apocalyptic to be real. Or that it wouldn't affect them in anyway if they just went about their lives.

Missouri was the same way. People seemed oblivious while my mind was going crazy with the extreme possibilities of where Covid-19 was heading. I felt like I was in a dream, moving through portals of oblivion while I was the only one who knew something dark was on the horizon. I wanted to scream at those who shrugged and moved on, but I kept my words to myself.

I just wanted to get home. I drove twelve hours, straight through with only stops for gas and bathroom breaks. My heart raced, my pulse pounded, and I developed a headache. No matter how I tried to calm myself, it made no difference. I knew bad things were on the way.

NPR had other guests on who tried to explain what they thought was happening. They took music breaks and played stories that were developed prior to Covid-19. I did not realize, until that trip, that after so many hours, NPR repeated the cycles of news, music, and stories. I think I listened to at least four rounds and every time I hoped to hear something different.

Once in awhile they would break in with an update, however by now, it was late and nothing new was developing. Still, NPR saved my sanity with their calm presence. No hysteria like other channels. No lies, only new information as it came to them. I relied heavily on NPR in the coming weeks to tell it like it is, not some made up version that others so desperately wanted heard.

I made it home to the saner and more grounded State of Illinois around 2 AM, exhausted but oh-so-happy to be safe and within my personal space with my husband. It was too late to check in with family members; that would have to wait until morning.

What we all believed, hoped for, prayed for, did not happen. The pandemic shut down everything for months. I feel our governor made the right decision in spite of the fact there were many who threw child-like tantrums of their 'rights' being taken away.

What rights? The right to die? To infect everyone around them? I could not comprehend this attitude, and it was directly within my family, divided right down the line of red and blue. After a while, that line blurred and became purple, and yet, those who remained firmly in the red got uglier and uglier. Families fought and split over what was the truth. Neighbors and friends stopped speaking to each other. Peaceful marches were attacked by white nationalist encouraged by politicians.

The United States divided once again, at each other's throats, fighting about this infection, denying the reality even as they took their last breath in an ICU. I am not a cryer, but I spent a good deal of time with tears leaking from my eyes. I claimed it was allergies, but in truth, it was grief.

Huge, unabating, debilitating, unbearable grief for my

fellow humans. For my country. For the world at large. And there were no answers, even when the vaccine came out because of this narrow view and lies told to the masses.

Blame was shifted. Violence erupted. Hostile groups attacked. Racism escalated. People died. At last count, August 2022, 1.03 million Americans have died. 6.43 million worldwide.

And still the deniers persist.

During those months of isolation, I learned how to use Zoom as I had to shift all my classes online. I edited and formatted five books for authors belonging to CHI. I wrote on my own books and created some brand-new classes beyond my own expectations. We took the Shamanic weekends to Zoom as well. I kept in touch with family and friends via Zoom and text.

I was learning new tools, new ways, and even cooking more since going out was not an option. The moment Latham and I realized how much money we saved not eating out was quite an eye-opener.

Sadness welled up again when I realized we would not be able to have our family holiday celebration. We always make the 'Christmas Lasagnas' for each family household, as well as for our gathering. The lasagnas became this huge deal when there weren't enough leftovers to send with everyone, so we started making and freezing whole pans of it for the kids. And then the grandkids who had their own places.

It's a LOT of lasagna. It takes us the better part of the day to create them all, and even with the pandemic, we continued the tradition. We joked that we would drive by each household and throw the frozen lasagna and

Christmas presents out the window and keep moving so as not to infect or get infected.

We did manage to deliver it all, and with masks on, hugged all our kids and grandkids as we stood in the cold.

More tears as the tragedy grew and grew. We didn't lose anyone in the family to Covid, even when some came down with it. However, I witnessed friends losing aging parents who were in nursing homes, or in the hospital ICU and they weren't allowed in to see them. The heartbreak as these friends realized their family members died alone.

No funerals. No memorials, no gathering of any kind.

The anger and frustrations grew. The blame was thrown around like mudballs, coating everything and everybody. The news was dreadful as obnoxious statements were made—still in denial—offering ridiculous and dangerous alternatives to either keep from getting the virus, or treat it, even though that too was killing people.

In the middle of this pandemic came the election, and the election deniers, promoted, once again, by hateful rhetoric. The United States became a world-wide symbol for insanity as our capitol was overrun by lunatics and an insurrection that we saw with our own eyes and heard with our own ears was denied. All manner of lies and foul statements fed the craziness.

We are still in the throes of this pandemic with the corona virus mutating over and over. Still, many refuse the vaccine, and poor nations who would give anything to have those vaccines and medications, don't and their people are dying in droves.

To this day, the callousness is overwhelming—the message seems to be, I'm fine and I don't care about you or your family. Hate is a palatable thing that lurks in the shadows, and I never know who will spew ugly words next. I find myself being careful of how I speak, the words I use in public, not because I am afraid to discuss it or defend my opinion.

No. It's because people have been murdered for less. Who has a gun tucked away and feels the right to 'defend' their point of view with a bullet between the eyes? The attacks on Asians, Blacks, and Hispanics are rampant. I fear for the sanity of my country. And like a trainwreck, I cannot look away from the news.

Roe v Wade fell. Fifty years and its gone. More insanity, more control, more lies and ugliness. I am overwhelmed AGAIN with grief.

The pandemic continues to tear the fabric of our lives apart. Just when we all thought it was okay to emerge from our homes and begin interacting in a normal, but careful, fashion, the virus mutates and spreads.

I chose to go to Teotihuacan, Mexico on an author's trip with twenty-eight other writers. It was wonderful, amazing, inspiring, and emotional. We went to the pyramids and did ceremony; we walked on fire and did Toltec shamanic journeying. We processed until we were blue in the face and danced with the Mayan troupe that graced us with their presence.

We did interviews for the collective book, Shaman Heart: Turning Pain into Passion and Purpose. We supported each other, and especially the new authors who were scared silly they weren't good enough to write a chapter. I heard personal stories that were heart-wrenching and yet those people smiled through their tears at the expressions of their sorrows.

Upon my return to the States, I came down with Covid. Everyone had something to say about it. You shouldn't have gone. Why weren't you more careful? Why did you go to a country like Mexico? I knew this would happen. You messed up everything. As you can see, many attempted a guilt trip, for whatever reason. Worried about me, or worried I would infect someone else, or worried that many things were cancelled while I did my ten days of isolation. Who knows.

I felt no guilt, and please believe me when I say that Mexico is not a third world country that ignores the health of their people. Everywhere we went, the sanitizing and caution was the main directive. One day we drove up into the mountains to visit Tolantongo hot springs, and at a rest stop we literally walked through an antibacterial spray. Everywhere we were required to use hand sanitizer and wipes. Mexico took care of us.

I believe I contracted Covid in one of the airports, Mexico City or Dallas. It was a mild case, and surprising in that I tested negative at 3 pm on Friday afternoon before a Shamanic event and positive at 7 am the next morning. Our event had to be cancelled.

I had a mild case, body aches, sore throat, and exhaustion, much like the 'regular flu'—something I never thought I would say. I slept a lot and drank a lot of water. I did not have an appetite, in fact, could hardly force food down but it only lasted a few days.

More and more people were coming down with the variations. Those who had the vaccination did far better than those who did not have the inoculation. I wish I could say I was surprised there were still virus/vaccination deniers, but I can't. There are still election deniers and insurrection deniers and, dear goddess, gun violence deniers.

I've asked myself a thousand times, why is this happening? When will it end? Will we ever come back to a sane, functioning nation? I wish I had an answer. As an avid history buff, even in the past 60+ years of my own life, I have seen the pendulum swing far to one side or the other. It always comes back to center at some point.

Hard times, and yet, our nation, and the world has seen worse times. We have overcome every possible thing thrown at us, and WE persist.

As an addendum to this whole story, I want to speak into the astrological viewpoint. Each 'Age' (Pieces is the most recent) lasts approximately 2,500 years. We are on the cusp of intellectual Aquarius pushing aside the emotional Pieces. There is no exact moment of when this begins or ends. It is all to do with Earth's rotation on its axis. The shift can take a good 100-200 years to complete.

Personally, I believe the dynamic began around the turn of the 20th century, and perhaps with the advent of the Industrial Age. I think we have been in the grip of these two enormous, clashing, confrontational energies who have no connection to humanity. They simply exist to bring about change.

Well, they certainly have, and I don't like it, lol.

Emotions run high in defense of personal beliefs and those in the vortex of resisting that same change. Others shrug and say, of course, this too shall pass and there's nothing I can do about it. Other factors fight dirty and do their best to destroy the values that we once all held.

We are a diverse nation, many cultures, spiritual beliefs, skin tones and ideals that set people apart. Each individual is free to speak their truth but not tear down the principles that has made the United States the strength that it is. I remain a loyal American and hope with all my heart we can heal from this pandemic as well as the vitriol that has torn us apart.

About the Author
Dr. Ruth A. Souther

Ruth Souther is a Metaphysical & Natural Arts practitioner in Springfield, IL. She is a Hypnotherapists, a Master Shamanic Breathwork Facilitator, Master Reiki Practitioner, Ritualist and Minister. She holds a Masters in Shamanic Intuitional Practices and a Doctorate of Shamanic Psychospiritual Studies through Venus Rising University.

She has written The Heart of Tarot (an intuitive guide to the cards); Vega's Path: The Elemental Priestess/Reclaiming the Elemental Priest (a year-long process), and three novels: Death of Innocence, Surrender of Ego and Rise of Rebellion. The fourth, Obsession of Love is forthcoming, as well as Vega's Path: The Universal Priestess.

Ruth is an Initiated Priestess through Diana's Grove and has taught with the Reclaiming Collective of San Francisco at Missouri and Texas Witch Camps. She has studied Tarot and Astrology since 1990, teaches many classes in both subjects, and provides readings both in person and online.

She created Vega's Path Priestess Process in 2012, designing it with her personal spiritual and elemental experiences as a guide. She is a facilitating member of of The Edge of Perception (public ritual/ceremony collective) and The Sanctuary of Formative Spirituality, a NFP church.

Ruth is a contributing author and board member/Chief Editor of Crystal Heart Imprints – an independent co-operative press that supports and guides both authors and artists in their creative projects. She is a facilitator/teacher at Naked Magik, an annual celebration of metaphysical practitioners, authors and artists.

Reach Ruth at 217-341-2768 or

ruthsouther52@gmail.com
www.vegaspath.com
www.facebook/vegaspath
www.formativespirituality.org
www.facebook/relaxedstateofmind
www.aaharaspiritualcommunity.org
www.crystalheartimprints.com
www.facebook/crystalheartimprints.com
www.nakedmagik.com

When will it end?

Chapter 7

What is Wealth?
A Year of Panic and New Riches

By T. L. Woodliff

"We have community spread, and now it is incumbent on us to do everything that we can to keep that from accelerating."

Community spread.

Those words landed in my stomach and pulled inward. Even as I shook my head, they took root. I wanted to drive them out of my world, back to those less developed countries across oceans, but could no longer do so. *It's real. It's here. Covid is here.*

The mayor's announcement forced our metroplex to accept that this mysterious plague pushing into our homes from some unknown land was now *our* reality. Up until those words were shared across T.V. stations and phone screens, it felt distant, and we safely landlocked Texans, untouchable.

I was at a large convention in Dallas, one that was drawing thousands of participants, when these words were blanketed over our metroplex of seven million. Shut it down. Get out. Go home. Touch no one. Touch nothing! Starting now.

I held back tears as my vending partner, Ruth, race for her car with her red curls drenched in the sudden downpouring of a Texas-gulley washer, her bags bulging from our desperate repacking: throw goods and personal items together into whatever luggage or box is at hand. She had almost a thousand miles to drive to get back to her home, to her people. But stores and shops were whisking people out the doors and shutting down. Would she even be able to find gas?

And what of our adventure? We were on a soul-healing and profitable journey at an international level. And I needed both. Crafting a holistic festival around two spiritual folk singers from Poland was our ultimate goal. The date was chosen. The singers were confirmed. The entire 29th floor of a hotel with floor to ceiling windows was ours. It was happening.

We decided to begin the adventure by vending and advertising at this large conference in Dallas. I remember checking my reflection in the mirror before entering the vending hall, my soft green eyes glowing with excitement for *change*. Eager. I smiled, savoring the feel of newly smoothed teeth that no longer held the metal brackets I'd grown used to over the last several years.

A new project, a straightened smile . . . And only a few months before, I'd wrapped up a book tour on the East Coast. A glorious high still danced through my veins— always the case after extended solo travel. I had finally,

finally, completed the goal I'd set as a small child: Become an author.

It was happening! I was reshaping myself in every way. And I knew that getting to Europe would be my next realized childhood dream. As I stood staring at myself in the mirror, I could almost taste the fresh buttery flavors of the Parisian croissant I was destined to enjoy. Or, perhaps, banger and mash in London.

But even with excitement shining, I could see the haunted look in that reflection; the etched marks of a shocked soul stretching out from the depths behind those eyes. The loss of my daughter had reshaped the story and available paths for myself and our whole family. Who we were was lost in a single moment. Where we would go, *could* go, was unknown.

Yvonne was only twenty-three-years-old, newly married, when a drunk driver took her away from us. My life as a dance teacher and at the farmers' market ended as we moved from Illinois to Texas to try and restart, unsure of exactly what that meant. (All these years later, I still have no idea.)

Our youngest child was just about to enter high school and we'd hoped the change would benefit all three of our surviving children. You can run away from grief, right? Just run far away?

It'd taken years for me to try and find any solid footing after the shock. I honestly no longer knew who I was, what I wanted or why I was even still on this planet—this stupid, stupid place that looked identical to the *right* world, the world where all of my children still lived. *How the hell did I get in this messed up twin realm?*

I turned to writing, something that was a bit of a desperate identity I'd formed as a small child—a belief I'd created that writing would be the thing to save me from poverty. The call to it was a siren's song to my young soul, crafted over long years of lean living.

Growing up poor in Oklahoma isn't really a rare thing; the state joined the Union late, almost sixty years after its neighbor, Texas, and never seemed to rally around the whole topic of wealth, even with oil. Not to mention, the majority of my neighbors were Cherokee, and the 'American Dream' was actually a 'nightmare reality'.

But I must admit to feeling envious as a small child in school, watching my peers with dark skin line up in the hallway at the snack counter of the small gym to receive the government checks they would take home to their families each month, and wishing desperately that I was one of them.

Don't get me wrong—I wasn't the only child with green eyes and light skin in the Cherokee Territory near the Arkansas border. There were no requirements for housing, so poor white people bought homes wherever they were available, wherever kin were close.

And the truth is, it wasn't the color of my skin or being counted among the poor in the poorest county in one of the poorest states that made me feel alone, isolated even when sitting in a crowded classroom. Among my large family and peers, my brother and I were the only ones without a dad at home, the children of abandonment.

Having one parent made the poverty seem more profound, somehow. It seems silly by today's norms, I know, but at the time, I stood out as an oddity, judged for something in which I had no control.

Mom did her best, but my brother and I felt the pangs of hunger and wore shoes with holes out into the rain. However, my grandparents gifted the world with fifteen children, so I had dozens and dozens of first cousins. Hand-me-downs were a welcomed occurrence and having to wear hole-filled shoes was more rare than common.

I graduated high school at seventeen and left town the same week to find work: I wanted to go anywhere I could find immediate income and started two jobs with all the side hustles I could fit in. I was writing short stories and sending them in, hoping writing would be the side hustle that would *take*. Money, and access to it, was my one focus.

Romance? I viewed the idea of falling in love at my age as an idiotic, temporary lapse in judgment that left you stranded, and I sneered as I watched friends and family alike marry before eighteen.

I, myself, made it all the way to twenty, thank you.

Besides numerous cousins, those grandparents also gifted us with fertile genes, it seemed. Marriage and divorce followed the birth of Yvonne in rapid succession.

You see, there was *an instinct* at play, one that told me life with the father of my child would not be free of financial difficulties. I'm not trying to say that he was a failure. He wasn't. But I grew to understand that he was weak where I needed someone strong. He was not a counterbalance to my own weaknesses. We weren't 'two peas in a pod' so much as 'two idiots with credit cards at the wrong time in history'.

We were too much alike in the wrong ways. Neither had any qualms about the whole '*buy now and pay later*' norm storming the nation in the 90s as American

manufacturing gave way to cheap, Chinese imports. It was
the first time such goods were flooding the markets as
Walmart kept up an expansion that would change our
country's identity from one that created goods to one that
imported cheap versions of them. It was heaven for we
service workers and college kids!

All the comforts I'd been denied as a child were now
at hand, accessible with that little piece of plastic I never
left home without, as instructed by a million
advertisements aimed at me all day long.

I knew it was a recipe for failure, and we divorced.
Cold? Yes. It was. He was hurt. I was scared of a life with
him and didn't know if I was strong enough to change
myself, let alone the both of us. He would have adapted to
any new focus I offered, but I realized I needed a partner
in life, not someone who would follow my lead down
whatever rabbit hole I discovered. And what I did know as
an absolute truth was that my little Yvonne would never
wear sneakers with holes in the bottom. Staying with him
made that a risk.

It was only after living together for a couple of years
that I realized it would all be on me. Every choice would,
ultimately, be my deciding vote, with little argument. He
was completely agreeable to whatever I wanted. It drove
me insane.

And I knew that with him alongside, my need to never
again 'go without' would be a disaster. So, I divorced him.

Shortly afterwards, much to my dismay, I fell head
over in heels in love with a man who was not rich. James
had oil-stained hands from his work on airplanes, a
deplorable lack of fingernails and a charming smile that
made my toes curl. I remember being annoyed that a look

from him would make my heart race. (Stupid heart.) His blue eyes looked like the summer sky, and when coupled with arms of steel and a tall, confident stature, parts other than my toes responded in a most pleasurable way.

And he was smart. He also came from what I considered the perfect stock—frugal parents, born during the Great Depression with a thrifty attitude. Even though his father had been a professor emeritus and director of student services at a good university, his mother was the kind who would buy regular potato chips, lay them out on clean kitchen towels and rinse off the salt instead of paying extra for the no-salt version. These people were my dream budgeters—money in the bank and wasting none of it!

While I finished school to earn my BA in literature, James worked hard, wisely choosing better jobs and denying some promotions, opting for the safer positions that weren't being culled during those crazy days of merges and corporate takeovers.

Most importantly, he paid the *maximum* amount of the company's matching retirement savings program with every paycheck.

This was our biggest argument, even with my overwhelming desire to live this path. We ended up raising four children on mostly a single income (I found ways to earn a little extra on the side as my ex-husband paid zero child support) and it was not easy.

Instead of new cars, James fixed whatever we had. No car was traded in before it had over 200,000 miles. I missed out on family vacations to the Great Lakes because I had summer work. We never made it to Disney World, like all the other children in our circle of friends. James and I never took romantic trips to Europe with just the two of us. We did without what seemed like normal expenses, at least in our suburban ecosystem.

I argued for a reduction in savings, just to be able to meet tough times or to do something extra. Would a trip to Chicago for the weekend with just the two of us be the end of the world? We'd scrimped and saved to take the kids to see the White Sox play the year they (eventually) won the World Series, and I wanted to explore more of that wild city with just my husband.

James argued against it. "We need to keep meeting the maximum amount they will match. That is the only thing that will save us, with one income." He stressed those last words and the look he gave me was a reminder of *my choice* to be, primarily, a stay-at-home mom.

Notwithstanding the work I did in the summers and on the side, I had made the choice of being there when the kids came home from school, of not making them the latch-key kid in the neighborhood, like I had been. I didn't want them to feel like everyone was staring at them, judging them, the way I had felt.

I made the right choice for our family, on that front. But about the money, James was right: save until it hurts and do without the extras.

Yet still, we had a blast. Yes, we didn't have new cars, but we took weekend road trips with the kids to campsites and state parks. We had a popup tent that we salvaged and repaired so we could visit all the quirky locations within reach, like Mark Twain's Cavern. (For weeks afterwards, whenever I passed one of our children in the hallway, they smelled of mosquito spray and damp earth, an *eau de caverne* original. Probably not available in your local boutique.)

But what made me most proud, two of our children were able to visit Europe through the foreign exchange programs! The child in me still stuck in the Cookson Hills danced for joy as she came to life vicariously. I may not have made it to Europe as a teen, but my kids did, damnit.

James once traded a case of beer for a 1950s Larson, a small speedboat straight out of a spy novel that just fit all six of us, and we boated and dragged bouncy things with a kid strapped in all summer long, each year. James and I snuck out a few times for a romantic boat ride with just the two of us, once the children were old enough to be left alone for a few hours. Yvonne enjoyed wickedly laughing as she rubbed her hands together whenever we pulled away, just to keep us on our toes.

But I still remember that first paycheck brought home where a tiny piece went to some distant future instead of being used to cover the ancient carpet in the house we'd leased, or to buy a mattress that first month of his new job in Illinois, instead of sleeping on a nest of sofa cushions.

And yet, those three digits in the retirement savings grew to four, then five, and up until it has more digits than seems believable. I want to see it all gathered in one spot, roll around in it for a while and then put it back to keep making new offspring. It's a great comfort to know we won't be hungry in our final years. Or rather, it was a comfort, for a few, short years.

Then the pandemic hit.

The convention my friend Ruth and I were attending in Dallas shut down with a single announcement from the mayor—no gatherings; close every business. I watched

Ruth's tiny form race for her car within half-an-hour of the notice. She didn't even stay for lunch, her panic taking hold and urging her to get back to Illinois while gas stations were still operating. We worried they would close as well.

I realized I was shaking as I drove home. I was finally beginning to reach the financial independence I'd always craved, and it was slipping away, once more.

We lived as frugally as ever. While I've never reached my mother-in-law's level of potato-chip-rinsing, I am that person who argues—in person—with the county that our property taxes shouldn't be raised just because the neighbors rubbed a genie's lamp and sold their home for above-market estimates.

But the closing down of airports, public events, even restaurants shook us to our financial core. My husband is in aviation. If people aren't flying, he can't earn an income.

"If we start moving any of our savings into the real world, we'll lose half in taxes!" James stood before me, far older than that muscular man who'd swept me off my feet in my twenties. His hair had grayed and was leaving his head entirely at an alarming rate.

Somewhere along the line he'd gain a lot of weight and carried it on his stomach. But his eyes were still those sky-blue beauties that made my heart skip. And when his wrinkly brow furrowed even more with worry, I was swept up in that emotion and replanted into my early years.

I knew he exaggerated. But the penalty rate for early withdrawal would be higher than the interest rate the money had earned in the previous year, at minimum, and then get slapped with a heftier income tax than it would have been when we made the money originally. Double whammy. If we pulled out any money early, a real chance of lean years lay ahead.

Meaning I now had to find a job *in that very instant*, even though millions of people had just been collectively fired. All of my upcoming book-selling events were cancelled. The schools where I had been doing substitute teaching were in shock, unsure of what they could do.

My instincts screamed at me to write: It was time to double down and write like a madwoman because people would be at home, and I could take advantage of the new e-book sales this *was sure* to generate.

But I was frozen. I couldn't wait the weeks and weeks it takes to craft something, find an editor and then began a book launch. I also knew tons of people who were suddenly without work, thinking it would be just for a few weeks, were heading to their computers to finally finish that novel they'd started years ago.

I homed in on the idea of working in grocery stores— they were still accessible. Even during a pandemic, people have to eat. There are some hard and fast rules that history has taught us during difficult times: People will need to eat, they will want something to do, and working for the rich turns out to be the best way to stay employed.

I got on the internet, did a little research, signed up for a grocery shopping and delivery service and started that same evening.

Those first days were insane. I received my orders via phone through the company with the exact items the customer wanted, and a limited ability to text them with any concerns or questions via some proxy text service.

There was nothing *but* concerns and questions as most of the items on all lists were simply *gone*. There was no water on the shelves. Toilet paper was horded faster than it could be made and disappeared by the third day with all the paper towels and facial tissues soon following. I spent the majority of my time taking pictures and texting people: **I'm sorry, but they have no ____. Would you like __ as a substitute?* It broke my heart when people were in desperate need of distilled water for their CPAP machines.

At first people were angry. "Why can't you find the pasta sauce I like? It's on the bottom shelf." I would send them a picture of the sign that showed where pasta sauces had once been displayed, and the clean rows of empty shelves that lay beneath that sign. The lack of pasta and macaroni and cheese seemed to cause the most outrage. Thank the gods the wine never ran out.

After a week of angry demands, the clients changed. They became kinder, ready to accept whatever close substitute I could find, if any. The pandemic grew worse as more people died; more people lost jobs. Frustrated clients turned to grateful ones when I showed them pictures of my gloved hands holding a rare pasta sauce I'd found in the uber-organic section of the market, pushed all the way back against the wall, for $7.99.

I claimed more than a few prizes (and great tips) on the deep, bottom rows by getting down on the floor and practically crawling into the dark cavern of a forgotten shelf. (I'm pretty sure I'll do okay in the zombie apocalypse.)

Twelve-hour days followed as more and most businesses shut down, large and small events were forcibly cancelled, and people went into home-hibernation. No one wanted to leave the safety of their four walls, not even for food.

Including me.

I wore a mask, a faceguard and disposable gloves. I tossed the gloves out as I exited the store and used hand sanitizer when I got in the car, after I took the groceries to the front door and knocked, and again before I entered the next store. The company policy had been to take the groceries into the house and put them on the counter, but I left them on the porch, rang the bell and walked back to my car to turn and wave once I was sure someone was home to take them in. They always were. And they always waved back, even that time I tripped on a step and faceplanted onto the front door.

As someone who ventured into public spaces, I was the potential bringer of death. I slept alone. I stayed away from my husband and children—the moment I walked in the door I went straight upstairs to our bedroom, now *my* bedroom and closed the door. I might see them in the back living room as I entered. If so, I'd cover my face, hold my breath, wave and then race upstairs. I texted them before I came home so they knew not to be in the entrance area.

I saw nobody outside of the stores. And while there, I kept far away from other shoppers. I didn't bother the grocery clerks to ask for items—if they weren't on the shelves, I presumed they were not available. I *did* ask about shipment days, but those were so screwed up by the end of the first month that the reliability of knowing when a truck would come was gone.

When items in high demand were delivered, the stock-people worked up a sweat. I watch as a bread delivery man, mask *and* faceguard in place, raced past the produce with his movable cart and then practically throw bread onto the shelves as he was needed in a million stores at once. When I returned to that same store later that evening, there were only a few loaves left because now everybody was eating three meals and all snacks at home. Restaurants that normally had no delivery option were just starting to get the word out that they were now using a service.

I thanked the bread man for getting there right when I needed him. He nodded and I could see his eyes were smiling when crinkles at the corners appeared. With faces masked, I was learning to read body language at boss level. It was the longest conversation I'd had in months.

It was getting to me.

Normally, I quite like being alone. Indeed, I crave it. A friend told me it's because I'm a double Scorpio. (Still not sure exactly what that means.) But not like this. Not walking for hours while staring at my phone, trying to handle orders coming in that can *in no way* be filled in the three-hour time frame, juggling the organization of my cart and car to handle three orders at once. The constant substitutions meant that I was mentally reshaping my route through the store with each text.

I was exhausted, and it turned out to be for no reason. Remember those three lessons of history I mentioned earlier? People need to eat, people will want something to do, and the third one: work for the rich as they won't feel the crunch of harsh times . . .

James' work in aviation had zero negative impact. He works with private planes, and if anything, those private planes were in high demand as the wealthy continued to travel from business to business or house to house or whatever they do. They had no desire to queue for limited commercial spots. Our savings account wouldn't need to be depleted.

But I was. I was totally depleted. And still, I didn't want to stop working, *just in case*. I know, not rational. But it was still there. *Keep bringing in extra money until this passes and we know we won't be homeless*. Completely irrational. I knew I needed to do something to shift my thinking.

Before the world came to a halt, James and I had talked about going west to St. George and spending a week hiking around the buttes. I reminded him that we still had the reservation. I could cancel it, or we could go. We should go, I argued. He said no, he didn't want *any* unnecessary travel. I mentioned that it was a place with no shared public spaces—it was its own townhome, accessible without going through a lobby. He still said no.

I looked at him, standing at one end of the hallway and me at the other, prepared to head upstairs, *again*, and stay in my room, *again*. He was dead serious. As I saw the stubborn set to his face and was now finding those blue eyes to be irritating, it dawned on me that my company was set up in Utah as well and I could work the shops there. I extended the reservation to an entire month and left without him, unsure about the reasons I was so intent on going, and not bothering to analyze them. I wanted *out*.

The drive was sheer magic. I've lived in the desert southwest, but I took roads never before traveled, stayed off the interstate and wandered through reservations and federal parks. The earth-carvings that wind and time have created of once-mountains still leaves me breathless. I usually drive 80 mph, but again and again I slowed down just to watch how sun and clouds changed the browns of bare earth into shades of mauve and burnt umber.

There are gentle curves in deep canyons that take an hour to finish a single bend. Then, you find yourself looking out over a great plain of sand and red stones, having somehow missed the fact that the road climbed upward as it turned. An open expanse seems interminable and yet changes shape and size as you round the next curve, swoop through the next canyon and rise into an endless sky.

After months of the monotony of moving from store to car to room, I could breathe. Mentally, I stretched to be in all that I could see. I felt free.

No, no that's not quite correct. I felt *untrapped*. Released.

The resort where I stayed was almost empty—I saw a few cars in the parking lot but I rarely saw another person. I worked a few stores, enjoying the longer drive times required in a small city with tall, twisting cactus and deep read earth all around. St. George is a clean, neat and trim little city that nestles on heaven's red-sedimentary doorstep. Living in the flat lands of North Texas after moving from the flat lands of Central Illinois, I'd forgotten the joy of not knowing what was around a wind-carved mesa until one got there.

I could have worked more often than I did. I should have written more often, too. But I took long walks and longer drives and just enjoyed allowing my eyes to stretch further than the shelf in front of me or the other side of the bedroom.

Then I decided to gamble and play the lottery a few towns to the east, in Kanab. It's a lottery I often played online—the monthly drawing to see if I might win a ticket, four months in advanced, and be allowed to hike in the federal park, Coyote Buttes, to visit The Wave.

If you could hear me say those words, *The Wave*, it would stretch with awe and no small amount of respect. I've wanted to visit Mother Earth's sandstone masterpiece for years. The layers of yellow, pink, white and red bands are wind and storm-carved into a small chute, hidden deep inside a wilderness of rock and mountain, reachable only by hiking for hours.

It's a strenuous route with challenging terrain. One must also use way-finding skills, looking for specific landmarks found only at certain angles as there isn't always a visible path on solid rock which is swept each day by wild winds.

Sandstone is delicate. They allow *only twenty souls a day* to travel into that wilderness. Ten are chosen by that online lottery, held four months ahead of the scheduled day.

And ten are chosen the day before, live in Kanab, which is still hours away from the entrance to the park. I had failed each and every time I did the online lottery. But I figured the drive would be another glorious stretch of colorful rock and earth, so I headed to Kanab.

I almost missed the morning lottery. Those were the pandemic days of 'all buildings shut tight' and while they were still holding the lottery, finding the right door was tricky. It was my own fault for following the signs. When I finally arrived at the backside of the building, I found people, and their cars, mixing near the door.

And I found a lot of people. Dozens and dozens. My chances were slim, and I'll get right to the end—I won the tenth ticket! Those first nine names called were nine shallow stabs of a sharp knife into my heart and I had absolutely no belief I would win—I'd never won the online, and I wouldn't win there. When he called my name, it took me a second to recognize it, and then I felt this grin stretch across my face that threatened to go all the way around my head as I looked up into a sea of disappointed faces. (Those same faces were lit with smiles when it was announced that, since I was solo, they would allow the rare option of one more ticket for two people to be drawn. My solo adventure gifted two extra souls a chance to see a miracle.)

The next morning, I headed out with my bag filled with five liters of water, energy bars, sunscreen and other things I thought I might need. The path started in a dry riverbed filled with red sand (that is still in my hiking boots, months later). It's funny, but I don't recall the feel of that riverbed under my feet. I think I was mentally flying so high that I could have walked barefoot on cactus needles and not noticed. I was going to see *The Wave*, live and in person!

The first hour was much like the trails around St. George, pleasurable and welcoming. Finally, I reached a wooden post with a sign that said everyone beyond must have the correct pass. In other words, no lottery losers beyond this point.

It's aptly named an undeveloped wilderness. There are no trees, just endless, upward jutes and buttes, canyons and sandstone. I walked with one foot higher than the other for hours, my feet pressed to the edges of my shoes.

I didn't see a single soul in the first two-and-a-half hours of walking. Standing on a mountain ledge made of rough-cut layers moving ever upward behind me, I stared over a deep canyon and across it to an even higher range, my view unobstructed for miles. The ledge I was on stretched forward toward the canyon for a long way before sloping sharply down, the same cuts of ragged layers slowly folding downward like thick cake batter poured into a sun-scorched pan, the edges burned and frayed.

It makes for an impressive, expansive view. Without being careful of keeping the landmarks in sight, the unmarked route would be easy to miss as the ledge itself *calls to the soul* for more exploration.

Alone, I never felt more comfortable. Humans have never lived in this range as it offers nothing to eat, and even less shelter. It is a space that exists as space, a beautiful thing in and of its unadorned self. The mixed colors in the stone and the fragile nature of each ragged edge of those layers tells the story of how ancient our world is, how tiny our time here.

As I neared the section called *The Wave*, I found other hikers. There were also volunteers and the first words I heard from another person without a mask in over six months were "Do you have your pass? What's your name?" They take this limit of twenty souls a day seriously.

Then I walked between two walls of sandstone and into the magical space. The volunteers made sure only one couple, or single hiker like me, had access to the majestic chute of Navajo Sandstone which seems to swirl in fat, long arches all around. My mind was so quietened by the space that I finally understood the word *sacred*. It front of me, it rose upward with waving lines and colors that seemed designed by a psychedelic acid trip. My whole body felt transported to a different world.

Just beyond the main chute was a narrow space with a ledge where I finally sat down, breathing it in. No one rushed me, just as I didn't rush those ahead of me. I touched as much of it with hands as I could, gentle so as not to brush away one single, precious grain. I breathed and felt whole. And finally, my mind relaxed.

You might think I wanted to linger, that one would be annoyed at having to give way to the next person, but that wasn't how it felt. It was an honor, a glorious gift, to be there for a few minutes. I understood that it would be enough to last me a lifetime.

The walk back had my feet pressing to the front of my shoes the entire way as I slanted downward for most of it. At one point my toes hurt so badly I wanted to take off my shoes and relax.

But then what? I had hours to travel to get back to my car. I was quickly going through all of the water I brought. If I took my shoes off, I would just have to put them back on as no one was going to carry me out.

It that moment, the pain went to a different part of my mind. It was the same place I had put hunger as a child. It's there, but it's an annoyance, something that can't be delt with right now and its importance is mitigated.

The last mile was almost too much for me. I had to stop and rest every hundred yards. At one point, I could see my car, but I stood in the shade of a small, brushy tree hanging over the dry riverbed trying to catch my breath.

I did make it to my car. I had a couple of adventures along the way that I don't have time to share here, and even one at the car itself. And a few days later I lost all my toenails. But still, that remarkable hike remains as vivid in my mind as if I had just returned.

When I finally *did* return home, I ceased working for the delivery service. Some people in restaurants and such had been out of work for months at this point, and it seemed selfish to keep a job we didn't need.

Despite my fears and my husband's concerns, we have enough. I am blessed beyond belief and am grateful that my non-perfect body still allows me such adventures. I would rather have more of such experiences than all the riches of retirement I thought we needed.

But what that journey gave me, more than anything, was a desire to let go of the need to define my new self. It is *in the moment* that all we have experienced is realized; the *now*. Into that sacred canyon I carried with me the memories of all whom I have ever loved, and just as a part of me shared in my children's journeys to Europe, I shared the hike with Yvonne, with all of them. I was myself, whole and defined by time and the space in which I dwelt.

About the Author
T.L. Woodliff

Terri is an accountability and writing coach living in the wilds of a major metroplex. She uses her MS in Applied Psychology to apply psychological interests to her characters in her novels, and to help others do the same. Her mantra is that every person has a story to tell, *and* the right to tell it, and she's devoted to helping people do just that. She is also a hypnotherapist, RTT Practitioner with certificates in editing, coaching and dance.

As a cofounder of The Witchf**kery of Writing programs, she's happily helping people discover and release the writer within. She is the president of the cooperative publishing house CHI (Crystal Heart Imprints) which is designed to help people learn about writing in supportive, productive and affordable ways.

Terri can be reached at:
www.TLWoodliff.com |
Terri@AnIntentionalThought.com

Chapter 8

You Don't Have to Get COVID-19 to Get Sick

The Physical Impact of Taking the Hippocratic Oath to Heart

By Sonja Glad, DPsS, LCPC

"Primum non nocere," from the Hippocratic Oath.
"First, do no harm."

I am by nature not a big worrier. If I were to guess, I'd say 90 percent of the people who know me would describe me as having a calm, peaceful energy. And about 90 percent of the time that's true.

Sure, I worry sometimes. Like everyone else in the world I know, I can get stressed. But by and large, I see myself as a calm, happy person. If anything, I tend to struggle more with depression than anxiety, except when it comes to my concerns over offending someone or hurting their feelings.

All of that changed in March of 2020.

My wife and I had plans to fly to Costa Rica for my nephew's wedding in mid-March. On March 12th, when we arrived at the airport, we noticed a few people wearing masks. We had heard about this whole coronavirus thing over in China, but at the time, it seemed like the problem was a world away. As an after-thought, I did bring a couple of scarves to wrap around our heads and over our mouth and nose areas while on the plane.

We arrived safely in Costa Rica on a Thursday and my sister picked us up at the airport in San Jose. The next day we started hearing about people cancelling their plans to attend the wedding. I felt so bad for my nephew and his wife and was glad we were there to support them.

They had gone to the courthouse the year before for their marriage license and were legally married, but this was the special event of which every bride dreams. The wedding was beautiful, and it was great spending time with my sister, her husband, their kids, and my two year old great-niece.

On Monday, at our request, my sister took us from the big city to the coast to one of her favorite beaches. You just can't visit Costa Rica and not go to the beach. The parking area was at capacity, which was unusual for a Monday.

My sister had heard rumors the government might be closing access to the beaches because of the coronavirus that was now spreading around the world, and people wanted to get in one last beach day. I know we sure did.

My sister suggested we Google 'beaches near us' and we discovered a wonderful beach spot where we walked along the shore, talked, and had a picnic. This beach had a very local feel to it with cars just pulled off the road right on the sand and garbage tossed here and there. No parking lots or attendants here!

It was beautiful and warm, the perfect Illinois winter escape. The palm fronds of the coconut trees gently swayed in the breeze, creating a rustling sound as the leaves brushed up against each other. As we walked along the water's edge, I felt the course sand exfoliating the soft winter skin from my feet.

"Don't you just love it here," I asked my sister.

"Yeah. It sure would be awful if the Costa Rican government really did close the beaches here. But that's a third world country for ya. Who knows what the government will do."

My sister and I simultaneously took a deep, cleansing breath and savored the salty ocean smells. Neither of us were sure when we would get another lung full of this uniquely wonderful scent.

On Tuesday, just five days after our arrival in Costa Rica, we were back at the airport. This time we saw tons of people wearing scarves, bandanas, and all kinds of different masks. I was glad I had brought two scarves. My wife said she felt lucky to be able to board the plane and head back into the United States.

I, in my usual way of being, was unconcerned. (However, it seemed like the border might close at any moment and, in fact, a few days later it did.)

Four days after our return, my world turned upside down–our governor shut down our state. Restaurants, hair salons and car dealerships closed their doors. Office workers of every type were instructed to work from home. Only essential workers like hospital staff and grocery store workers were allowed to go to work. The rest of us were instructed to stay home unless it was an emergency.

I am a psychotherapist by trade and self-employed. I had to scramble to turn my in-person, office based practice into a telehealth therapy practice. Being self-employed, I have to work, or I don't get paid. At that time, there were no unemployment benefits for self-employed workers like me.

As a side note, I was the diametrical opposite of a computer geek (whom I highly respect and value). I knew how to access a few things like email and how to write reports and such on my computer, but otherwise, I was computer illiterate.

Sitting in front of my computer, I felt immobilized by anxiety. I had Skyped before but never done anything like this for work, and for work, the perfectionist in me always wants to do my best. Just the thought of doing something unfamiliar and possibly not being good at it, freaked me out.

Will I be able to notice the subtle nuances over video or the phone like I can observe when I'm sitting across the coffee table from clients?

I heavily relied on using all of my senses when working with my treasured clients.

But slowly I learned.

At first, I 'saw' my clients over the phone. I soon learned about a HIPPA compliant platform called doxy.me and started counseling folks through that portal. At least I could see them, unless my internet connection was poor, in which case we'd use the phone.

To say I was frequently frustrated would be an understatement of grand proportions. Daily I struggled with getting connected to the internet and keeping that connection strong. I feared the regular interruptions were detrimental to the therapeutic process.

Who wants to have to reboot their computer system right in the middle of telling their therapist about a traumatic experience they had just had?

I had to cancel our April trip to Florida, where I was supposed to take my goddaughters, Sanaia and Myara, for Spring Break. They were disappointed, which hurt me, as I hate letting my loved ones down. It was Myara's senior year of high school, and she had been so excited to lay out in the sun on Daytona Beach.

Instead of working the week of Spring Break 2020, I decided to design and build a small 12' x 14' sanctuary on our farm property. I had been thinking about doing something like this for several years but had never had the time. Now it seemed like all I had was time.

Fewer client sessions. No vacations. No going out to eat or socializing with friends. No running errands and getting distracted at the craft store. This project took months and helped me stay focused, fit, and not gain those COVID 19 pounds everyone else seemed to be gaining.

It also gave me an excuse to get out of the house and go shopping for supplies at the hardware store as hardware store workers were considered essential workers.

Three months later, in June, I was able to reopen my office. Mental health therapists were now considered essential workers. I was so happy to see my clients in person again. I hadn't seen some of my clients in months as they had not been comfortable with technology or were spending their entire work day on the computer so hadn't wanted to take advantage of telehealth.

Some of my clients preferred the telehealth option, so I turned my practice into a hybrid one, seeing clients both in-person in the office and on-line from home. This also worked well for my office mate, who due to health issues and age was in the high risk category.

We didn't need to be concerned about crossing paths as she used the office on Mondays, Tuesdays, and Thursdays while I used the office on Wednesdays, Fridays and Saturdays. There were a few hiccups at first, but we adjusted quickly.

While I loved being face to face with my clients, it was also stressful.

What if I have COVID-19? What if I give it to my client? What if my client then passes it on to someone else and they end up in the hospital, or worse? What if my client has COVID-19 and my next client gets it from them? How do I balance my desire to see my clients face-to-face with my personal axiom of "Do no harm"?

Daily temperature checks. Mask and shield covering the face. Sanitize, sanitize, sanitize. *Can I still smell things? What if I'm asymptomatic? Is this headache a symptom of COVID-19?*

I found myself in a constant state of worry.

I struggled with getting to sleep and staying asleep. The traditional sleep aides either didn't work or left me feeling so groggy the next day it wasn't worth taking them. I knew the constant stress was bad for my mind, body and spirit so I kept working on doing things to counterbalance the stress, like regular exercise, working on my sanctuary project, and speaking with my friends on the phone.

After a lot of research on the medical benefits of cannabis for sleep, I tried several different cannabis products: CBD gummies, then a tincture, then a combination of CBD, CBD-N, and THC. I took these intermittently in small doses and found them to be helpful for sleep, without feeling the groggy hangover effect the next day.

While previously not being opposed to cannabis, I rarely smoked it. I had chosen to get high on things like hiking and being creative instead of using marijuana. Now I used edibles as medicine for sleep.

I learned new coping strategies for anxiety and used them regularly. One particular coping strategy I really liked was called tipping. Basically, I would bend forward from a standing position and try to get my head lower than my heart and count to 30.

This is supposed to reregulate a person's autonomic nervous system, which gets activated when one's body thinks it's in danger. (Try it the next time you are having a physical response to your anxious thoughts. Make sure you stand upright slowly, or you may feel dizzy.)

Less than two months after reopening my office, after canceling my trip to Florida with my god-daughters, then being forced to cancel my trip to Hawaii for a mental health training and my trip to Scotland with a friend, I booked a flight to go see my parents.

I hadn't seen them since Christmas and knew my opportunity of getting to spend time with my father was getting short. His mind and body were rapidly declining between the

Alzheimer's and Parkinson's diagnoses. Again, I questioned myself. *Is it more important to visit my parents or do I avoid going as I might bring them harm?*

One day before my scheduled departure, on July 24th,

I didn't feel well. I had worked all day and had made numerous trips to the restroom. As the day progressed, I felt worse and worse.

Should I get tested? Surely I'm fine. What if I have COVID-19 and give it to my parents?

That was the clincher for me. On my way home from work, I stopped at the recently established testing site on 6th Street in Springfield, just a few miles from my office.

"Do you have a fever or chills?"

"No, I don't think so," I replied.

"Cough, shortness of breath, or difficulty breathing?"

"Well, I have shortness of breath and a sore throat," I croaked.

"Fatigue, muscle or body aches?"

"Yes, but it could be from something else. I haven't been sleeping well."

"Headache?"

"Yes."

"Loss of taste or smell?"

"No."

"Sore throat, congestion or runny nose?"

"Well, yes, my throat is sore," I repeated.

"Nausea, vomiting or diarrhea?"

"Nausea and diarrhea," I say as my level of anxiety ratcheted up.

The screener at the emergency testing site then said, "Please put on your mask and go ahead and park in an open parking spot. Call the number on the sign, and we'll get you registered to be tested."

OH CRAP! This is for real. I must have enough symptoms that warrants my being tested. I hope I get the results before my plane leaves tomorrow.

138

THE CHAOS OF COVID

Someone in full protective gear approached my car window, which I rolled down. She confirmed my identity then inserted the swab up my left nostril and tickled my brain. This tickle gave me tears of pain, not tears from laughter.

"When will I get the results?"

"You should get them in two to three days," she told me.

"But I have a plane to catch tomorrow." My eyes pleaded with her for understanding.

"I'm sorry, but you'll need to cancel your trip and quarantine until you get the results. The airlines are pretty good about rescheduling. I hope you feel better soon," the kind woman said. She then handed me some Kleenex and several pages of information and went back through the tent opening that was in front of the medical building.

I felt stunned. *How could I have gotten COVID? I do almost everything I'm supposed to. We did go out for dinner a few nights ago, but we kept our masks on unless we were eating, and we sat outside.*

I went home, told my wife and called the airline to cancel my trip.

With a heavy heart and trembling hand, I called my parents. I knew they would be disappointed and disappointing them was the very last thing in the world I wanted to do.

"Hi, Mom. It's Sonja."

"Oh, hi Sonja! We're so excited you're coming tomorrow! Glenn, it's Sonja on the phone," my mother called out to my father. "I've been telling your Dad for weeks you'll be visiting soon. Your daddy can't wait to see you! He keeps asking when you are coming, and we've been doing a count down."

As she took a breath I said, "Well, Mom, that's why I'm calling." I paused. "I have some symptoms of COVID-19, so I went to get screened to see if I was eligible to get tested, and well, apparently I have enough symptoms to warrant being tested. Then they told me I had to quarantine until I get my test results which won't be until Monday or Tuesday. So..... I've had to cancel my flight. I won't be coming tomorrow."

"Oh, no, Sonja! Glenn," my mom called out, "Sonja won't be coming tomorrow because she's sick and has to quarantine."

"What do you mean she has to quarantine?" I heard my dad asking in the background.

"You've seen the news, Glenn. There are a lot of people all over the world that are sick. It's a pandemic. You know, the corona virus."

"And Sonja has it?" my dad asked.

"We don't know for sure she has it but the doctors told her she has to stay home until she finds out."

"But she's supposed to come see me tomorrow," I heard my dad's voice crack and my heart felt like a giant hand was squeezing it.

"I know honey, but she can't come if she's sick. We would hate for her to bring the virus here and give it to someone."

My mother returned her attention to me. "So when do you think you'll be able to come for a visit?"

"I don't know. I guess it will depend on whether or not I have it. And you know I'm supposed to go camping with Susan and the boys," I say, referring to our upcoming camping trip to Michigan with our camping buddies. "But

I'll schedule something as soon as I possibly can. I'm so sorry, Mom."

"Oh well, it can't be helped. It's a crazy world we live in. So what exactly are your symptoms?"

I described my symptoms, asked how they were doing, apologized again, and hung up.

Tears of sadness, and relief, streamed down my face. My wife held me as I cried into her shoulder with my mask on. "I hope we don't have to cancel our camping trip, too," I blurted out as a whole new spurt of tears started flowing.

"Honey," my wife said soothingly. "It'll be okay. I don't care if we don't go camping."

"But I do," I wailed. "We haven't hardly gotten to do anything this year." My wife continued to hold me and stroke my hair. "You shouldn't even be near me," I told her as I moved six feet away and removed my soggy mask.

We made plans for how we would quarantine separately together until I received the results. "If you have it, I probably have it already," she insisted.

"But if you don't, we need to err on the side of caution. I sure don't want to give it to you if you don't have it," I insisted. Again the thought, *Do no harm*, ran through my mind.

The next day I felt better! No sore throat. No shortness of breath or headache. No nausea or diarrhea. *Could my symptoms have been from anxiety of exposing my parents to COVID-19?*

The following day I received the results of my COVID-19 test. The result was negative. I believe all my COVID-19 symptoms were anxiety based. The anxiety of sharing COVID-19 with another person and thus harming them had made me physically ill.

A month later, with similar symptoms, I boarded a plane to Florida to go visit my parents. As I struggled to breathe beneath my double layer of masks and my full face shield, my mantra became:

You're okay. This is just your body's response to your anxiety. You're okay. This is just your body's response to anxiety. You're okay. This is just how your body is responding to anxiety. You can do this. Goodness knows you don't want to disappoint them again.

Once I arrived to my parent's retirement community, I had to check in with the nurse responder who took my temperature and asked me some health related questions. I had to check in daily with the nurse responder. And every day, I was okay.

While there, I continued my self-care habit of daily walks. On campus, I was restricted from entering any of the public buildings, including the post office. Even walking outside, I had to don my mask. My favorite mask for exercise breathability, at the time, was one I had constructed from an old exercise sock, based on directions from an AARP article.

I cut the toe end of the sock off then cut along the top edge of the sock. Next I opened up the sock and cut little slices at each side to loop around my ears. The heel of the sock then rested comfortably over my nose, mouth, and chin. Looking back now, it's laughable. Sure I could breathe through it, but I'm pretty sure tiny virus molecules could navigate their way through the single layer of material as well.

I'm so grateful for the opportunity to have made that trip to visit my parents, as it was the last time my dad and I were able to have a real conversation. When I visited next, just two months later, I noticed his dementia had become significantly more pronounced.

I took him to an outdoor restaurant called The Deck Down Under which is under the Dunlawton Bridge in Port Orange, Florida. His mother had lived in South Daytona Beach for most of my childhood and a good portion of my adulthood. We had visited the beach and this restaurant many, many times over the years. He enjoyed what turned out to be his last full-octane beer to go with his fried shrimp, coleslaw, and fries.

At the restaurant, we experienced the kindness of strangers. This has been something I regularly encounter. A nice man opened the door to the men's room and guarded it while I pushed my dad in his wheelchair into the handicapped stall and helped him use the toilet.

While driving home, I asked him how he was doing with the aging process. He told me he no longer felt joy in life. It seemed the couple dancing in the yard outside his window was more real to him than what was actually going on in the world. He really didn't seem to have much understanding of the pandemic and couldn't put a mask on himself nor understand why he needed to wear one.

It was while on this trip to my parent's retirement community that I saw what would become one of the most heart wrenching pictures that has remained in my mind as a representation of these pandemic years. While I was out walking in the community, I happened to look over to my left as my gaze followed a butterfly.

Off in the near distance, I saw an older woman standing outside one of the nursing care facilities knocking on a big plate glass window. She cupped her hands around her eyes as she peered through the window. Then she knocked again. I still tear up every time this image comes into my mind.

When I returned to my parent's duplex from my walk, I told my mother what I had seen.

"They're quarantined in that building," my mom said. "And her husband was probably in there. Maybe now you can see why I don't want to put your dad there. I wouldn't get to be with him. And I promised him I would take care of him."

Six months later, on another visit, we ended up moving my dad to the Memory Care building, as my mother, at age 80, was no longer able to care for him safely. Fortunately, we were able to visit with him after following the protocol of signing in, taking our temperature, and wearing our masks while there.

He was there for six months before he died. For part of that time, my mother could only see him for 15-20 minutes each day, in a special sanitized room with a plastic partition between them. My mom told me my dad would stretch out his leg under the table with the partition on it and she would rub his foot.

This was their way of communicating their affection for one another and connecting without words. I was stunned that this brilliant, multi-lingual financial powerhouse couldn't complete a thought.

I am eternally grateful that I was there, on another planned visit, and able to help feed my dad his last meal. That was on November 1st, 2021. I didn't know it at the time, but that evening he spoke the last words I would ever hear him speak.

I don't remember what they were, just that he was expressing interest in my travels and my life. He seemed to have come to a place of resolution regarding his frustration of not being able to finish a sentence. I knew he was glad I was there.

I wondered if he knew my prayer for him was, *May he be released from suffering.* I feel he waited for my arrival so when he died, I would be there to support my mother.

By November of 2021, I was fully vaccinated and had had my first booster shot. My parents were also fully vaccinated and had just received their first boosters. I thought we were all safe. My father seemed to be stable.

And then he wasn't.

At first, I thought he was sleeping in as he had had a rough night. It wasn't until later when the incredibly kind and caring staff at the Hagen Memory Care Facility told us they were calling in a hospice nurse to sit with him overnight that we realized something wasn't right. The next day, one of the hospice workers taught me how to use the little round sponges on a stick to wet his lips and the inside of his mouth.

I sat with my dad off and on for the next five days as he transitioned. I am so very grateful that I could sit at his bedside, holding his hand, and that the level of caution was not like it had been the month before when my mother could only see him in the special, regularly sanitized room for only 15 minutes a day.

There are so many big and little COVID-19 stories we each have. The up side for me was the fact that my traveling adventures were much less costly than in previous years. This made it possible for me to set aside quite a bit of money for my future.

Instead of traveling abroad, I enjoyed visiting several national parks like the Grand Canyon and Saguaro NP in

Arizona. I also visited Pictured Rocks National Shore and the Apostle Islands in Michigan and Wisconsin. There were also two wonderful trips to Virginia both to Williamsburg and Shenandoah NP.

Sometimes, I have to remind myself that the pandemic wasn't all bad. I learned how to navigate the whole telehealth process, which will continue to serve me in the future, as I am now able to see clients from anywhere in the world.

I feel the biggest lesson I'm taking away from the past two years of the pandemic is coming to terms with this whole *Do no harm* belief system I've had since I was just a little girl.

As the oldest female child in the household, I felt responsible for taking care of my mother when she was sick, my sister so she would stay out of trouble, and my dad's emotional happiness. These past two years amplified this sense of responsibility and showed me the physical consequences of carrying this load of responsibility.

My anxiety related to my fear of making someone sick, which required my following all the rules and guidelines to safeguard others, had taken quite the toll on the health of my mind, body and spirit. In the process, I let my own happiness and peace of mind take a backseat.

In January of 2021, I was having heart palpitation and tightness in my chest. My nurse practitioner set me up with a heart monitor, which I wore for two weeks. The results showed I was fine.

I still struggle with not wearing a mask, yet it feels like I'm trying to take care of others who don't seem to care about me taking care of them, as evidenced by their lack of wearing a mask. So, for now, I will continue to wear a mask to protect myself and others.

In a way, the past two years have prepared me for my future where my focus is not on being attached to the expectations of others, nor doing for others at the cost of my health and happiness. Instead, I'm focusing more fully on my self-care and following where my heart and Spirit guide me. I'm learning to first do no harm to myself.

Mahalo nui loa!

About the Author
Sonja Glad

Sonja Glad, DPsS, LCPC has a remote mental health private practice, as she has replanted her roots from living in Central Illinois to spending some time in Hawaii. Her focus is on working with people who are in the process of making life changes, or who are seeking personal/spiritual growth.

Sonja recently earned her Doctorate degree in PsychoSpiritual Studies. She is a Shamanic Minister, a Reiki Master, a Breathwork Facilitator, and a Soul Collage Facilitator.

In 2021, Sonja's first children's book was published, *WooHoo For Sensitive Somjay*. Sonja is making a career shift and is excited to have more time for writing and illustrating future children's books.

In early 2022, Sonja participated in her first book collaborative, *Shaman Heart, Turning Pain Into Passion and Purpose* with lead author Stephanie Urbina Jones.

Sonja is happiest when she can be outdoors. She loves reading, writing, being creative, working on personal growth, hiking, snorkeling, kayaking, whitewater rafting, and exploring the world. Of course, doing outdoors things with a good friend puts the cherry on top of fabulous.

Learn more about Sonja:

On her website:
www.sonjaglad.com

On youtube at:
https://www.youtube.com/watch?v=qtZHo0NkJ5o

Find her books at:
https://www.amazon.com/WooHoo-Sensitive-Somjay-Sonja-Glad/dp/1945567279/ref=sr_1_1?keywords=WooHoo+for+Sensitive+Somjay+by+Sonja+Glad&qid=1642442490&sr=8-1

And:
https://www.amazon.com/Shaman-Heart-Turning-Passion-Purpose-ebook/dp/B09X8DH7SN

I'm okay; I'm okay.

Chapter 9

Jumping the Line Between
Anger and Madness:
Diving Down the COVID Rabbit Hole

By Michelle Angone

I did not have COVID three times. Then again, maybe I did. To be quite honest, I really do not know if I had it three times or not and neither does anyone else. I mean there is a logical explanation for this. There isn't anything mystical or special about any of it.

In fact, most of it was just plain stupidity. Some of the stupidity was mine, I won't claim innocence, and a whole lot of it was all that medical science everyone started treating like religion. Nothing like the word pandemic to put the fear of Florence Nightingale into you.

Let's start at the very beginning.

The first time I didn't have COVID was in late January of 2020. Of course, I didn't have COVID, no one could have had COVID at that time, right? Well, not exactly. Have you ever seen that episode of Rick and Morty when the entire planet got infected with a world destroying virus because of a school dance?

My story is kind of like that. On January 19, 2020, my youngest daughter attended her first homeschool dance. The thing about homeschool dances is that they pull kids from a large radius. I just happen to live in the North Atlanta suburbs and our population is in a perpetual state of growth.

This means we had a lot of kids from all over the Atlanta metro area at the dance. Another thing homeschoolers have is a lot of two parent homes that include a homeschool parent and one that usually travels a lot for work.

It was January, and some kids had the sniffles, some had popped some ibuprofen and elderberry and attended their first middle school dance without a second thought.

There was one thing no one knew at the time. A dad had recently returned home from a trip to Asia. I could say it was China, but that would be a lie, I don't remember where he had been.

I just remember we all blamed him later. He became our personal patient zero. The kids got sick first. There were a lot of cancelled events and clubs the week following the dance. Homeschoolers have standing rules about keeping your sick kids home.

We are a group of flexible people who have gone into lock downs over the flu long before it was fashionable, or mandated, or whatever. There were sick kids at that dance. We all saw them, and no one did a thing about it. Frankly, it was January and it had already been a long school year. Sometimes you just live a little dangerously, I guess.

My daughter was the first to go down in our house. Not

a big deal. We gave her tomato soup, 7-up, and let her watch Netflix for hours on end. It was odd that her immune system that normally can't handle a cold just bounced back from her bout with the crud so fast.

All was good until I got it. I got the headache, the chills, weak limbs, and the dreaded cough. There was not a rock the couch option for me. I went to bed and tried to sleep it off. It didn't matter how hard or how long I coughed, I was determined to sleep the bug away.

Sleeping away a bug when you can't stop coughing is nearly impossible, in case you are wondering. I resorted to popping three cough drops at a time and going to sleep with them in my mouth. You know, sleeping with something in your mouth you could choke to death on. It was one of the grossest illnesses I had in decades.

No woman in her late 40's who had birthed four children wants to be bedbound and coughing up a lung for days on end. It seemed like forever but was probably more like a week and a half before my fever broke. Perhaps it was another four days before the coughing cleared up and my cough drop dependency weened down to one at a time.

Now I could watch television and listen to the news or what was passing as news at the time. There was this corona virus thing all over Europe and had landed in the United States. The daily press briefings were no less than terrifying.

My brain couldn't help but think of all those things that were going to kill us in the past several years. I was starting to get real Ebola vibes, except this was not the killer disease of the year season which tended to line up with my seasonal job in September for a few years running. No, this was off script being February and all.

The symptoms got to me the moment I heard them. I heard fever, chills, body aches, cough.

Hold up, I think I just had that!

So that's when I convinced myself that I had already had the plague. If I had the corona virus, then that meant I had antibodies, and that meant I was immune. Yup, that was my professional diagnosis from a year of nursing school a few decades back. Because logic and medical science, the one we are supposed to trust, did say that my theory was true.

The exception being that I had never been exposed to anyone who knew for sure they had corona virus. It was all purely coincidental. I believe there are no coincidences. I had obviously won favor with the gods, universe, whomever, but who cared? With the powers of mind over matter, I was immune and proceeded to go on with my life.

In March of 2020 the entire country went into what is affectionately referred to as lock down. Our family was living a bit outside of the norm, both by choice and by circumstance. My pregnant daughter and her husband had recently moved into our basement, and we were in the middle of installing a bathroom for the two of them.

Thankfully the home improvement stores were deemed essential because we were at each of them two to three times a day for a couple of weeks. We saw the lockdown as a nuisance and something to be envious of. We would have loved to have experienced the nationwide quarantine, but we had a toilet and tile to install.

It sounds like we were lackadaisical about the killer pandemic, but that isn't exactly true. We had both a registered nurse working in a hospital and a sheriff's deputy living under our roof. If the virus was going to make its way to anyone, it was going to be our household.

We did our part. We religiously washed our hands and kept up with the mask on, mask off debate the best we could. If we are being fair, I'd say we were a very safe family to be around, if we could have been around anyone outside of our household that is. The reality was that we as a family were in constant risk. We could live in a state of absolute fear or just you know, live.

Don't get me wrong, we watched the crazy tiger man and his crazier nemesis just like everyone else. As a family of six with a dog and a cat, we also had to make sure our family was taken care of. We stood in line for toilet paper. In fact, one day my daughter and I went to three different warehouse stores in one day to stock up on toilet paper.

Driving twenty-five minutes to get from location to location just doesn't mean that much to you when you live in Atlanta. It wasn't that bad considering how few cars were out on the roads. I won't lie, the line standing got to me.

If you were near, you could hear my cold war era history lesson. I recalled seeing photos of people in the USSR standing in line for toilet paper. I remember asking myself if they knew they were lacking freedom. I decided the Russians had no idea considering everyone in line around me seemed perfectly fine just waiting.

It was like they had been doing this their entire lives, but it was my first time. Why was everyone just so content with the 'new normal?' Better yet why was I so angry about it when everyone else was going with the flow?

My first push over the edge was caused by standing in all those lines trying to get toilet paper and buying a freezer full of meat just in case the shit hit the fan. It really is not the place for a person who really enjoys a good conspiracy theory. I am not one of those people who believes in all the conspiracies, but I do enjoy learning about them.

Call it my guilty pleasure. I grew bored of regular television years ago when I fell down the proverbial YouTube rabbit hole. I mean YouTube used to be the place for all things conspiracy. I'm not talking JFK here. I'm talking alternative histories, Flat Earth, Hollow Earth, Flat Hollow Earth, lizard people, giants, giant lizard people, shape shifters, secret societies, shadow government, chem trails, simulation theory, it just goes on and on and I love it all. I take pride in being able to talk the talk with nearly everyone about anyone of the crazy theories out there.

Standing in line for an hour noticing how vastly different people were acting not only in front and behind me but from location to location was eye opening. One lady wore a hazmat suit. If you were me and you knew a lot about so many weird things, you may have started to get a few ideas, just like I did.

I live in the city that famous zombie show started out at. The CDC is right here. Thankfully I had a zombie survival guide on my bookshelf. I'm sure my sister thought it was a gag gift when she gave to us. Ha!

It was going to be my lifesaver once the power grid went down. I really needed to cut back on videos before I started believing those alphabet drops everyone was talking about.

There was the great glove debate at first, or maybe it was just around here. I have a good amount of medical training. I did attend nursing school even though I didn't finish. I remember the simple things, like how to use gloves. It was obvious to me that there were very few medical staff out and about during the day with me. The people around me had absolutely no idea how to use gloves properly.

"Becky, please take off your dirty gloves before getting in your car."

"Hey Bob, do you mind not throwing your gloves on the damn ground before getting into your electric car?"

"Reba, did you really just touch your face with the glove you just manhandled everything in Kroger with?"

Yeah, the gloves really got to me. It didn't last long. Soon enough every adult discovered hand sanitizer for the very first time. It was as if they had never purchased ten bottles of hand sanitizer on the first day of school for a third grader. No surprise that most of these people didn't realize hand sanitizer was a neurotoxin.

I would watch them rub half a bottle on their hands and then pop a breath mint in their mouths not two seconds later. I worried for those people. Would they live long enough to catch the dreaded plague? Perhaps it was the survival of the fittest we had heard so much about back in elementary school.

I know it sounds like I was just living my happy little secluded or not secluded life, but honestly it wasn't like that. You know what though? I never cleaned out a closet, not one. I didn't get on that clean and purge wagon that everyone else did.

I didn't learn to bake bread. Why would I? I have gluten issues after all. I read a lot. I'm pretty sure I watched all of YouTube. But I never exercised or dieted. I guess I just went back to those latch key kid days of the 1980's and did my thing.

I became a Nana for the first time and our family revolved around that little guy for so many months that if it hadn't been for all the 'news' I think we would have forgotten all about COVID. That is until my son-in-law caught it at a training class.

He got the flu like symptoms and my daughter took the baby and slept in a different room. They had moved out at this point, but we were all together so often it didn't matter. We locked down tight during this time. We are not reckless or uncaring. We did understand that the wrong person could become quite ill or even die from this thing.

I had my first COVID test. I was expecting it to be a bit more unpleasant than it was. No one seemed overly concerned or cared at the testing shed. They made jokes about how far up I tried to shove the swab. In and out in seconds flat and fifteen minutes later, I was negative.

The next day I couldn't taste a thing. I felt completely fine, I just couldn't taste anything. I could smell which was odd without having the ability to also taste. My daughter both tested negative and lost her sense of taste as well. We were the only two people in our two households who were affected with the taste thing.

There were lots of talk at one point about the rapid COVID tests having a fifty percent fail rate. That was it then, we were victims of the fail rate. There really wasn't a reason to quarantine from each other. We figured if one person had it, then everyone was sure to catch it.

Once my son-in-law felt up to it we had a family cookout. The men cooked the steaks, and the women cooked the sides, just the way the gods intended. Of course, Loki may have had a hand in our cooking adventures.

THE CHAOS OF COVID

We had those little new potatoes coated in olive oil and coarse salt. The potatoes went into a bag, and we shook the salt in long past when our ancestors begged us to stop. Shake, shake, shake, and into the oven they went. Oh, the glorious smell of the food that night. Everyone was ravenous and dug in the second they sat down.

Then with a collective cough and gag everyone sans my oldest daughter and I coughed and gagged. I'm not sure what the lethal dose of salt is, but my family is quite certain we were dangerously close to eating it. The amazing thing is, my daughter and I could taste the salt on those potatoes.

We happily ate two servings each while everyone else threw theirs out. I am certain the salt potato fiasco will become legend in my family and one day my great-grandchildren will hear stories of it.

It felt like months before I could taste again although it was probably weeks. I craved salt, but I think that it was just because I could taste it. I know I ate a lot of French fries and potato chips during that time. It may have been the only thing I ate if I look back honestly.

Not being able to taste is one of the strangest things that has ever happened to me. Yet, according to my rapid COVID test I did not have COVID, and it was all just a fluke with strange timing. So many coincidences but I've already voiced my thought on those. That was the second time I didn't have COVID.

Time went on, the way time does.

Thanksgiving came and went. The baby had his first birthday and there was another baby on the way. Soon it was Christmas again. I had a big Christmas and ordered a good ninety percent of the gifts. I shopped early and had everything exactly the way I wanted.

There was an abundance of food, piles of gifts, and everyone stuffed the stockings. The world was back to normal, and I was in heaven. We worked out new traditions around my daughter's family. My son was home and other than the cold my soon to be son-in-law had it was wonderful.

It was over all too soon, but that was okay because it just a week or so we would be visiting Illinois for the first time since 2019. My mother-in-law was finally going to meet her great-grandson. We had made it!

But wait, we are not finished yet. The day after my son flew home I started to feel a bit run down. I wish I could tell you what day this was, but I've lost a bit of time from this period. One day I had a bit of a headache, the kind you get when you are a little bit dehydrated.

I was tired, not just sleepy. I was straight up exhausted. I went to sleep and then all the days started running together. Hour by hour and moment by moment my lungs just didn't want to work anymore. Here's the thing, I had no fear of anything bad happening to me. I knew I was not going to die no matter how much my body was telling me it needed oxygen.

I would wake up and will air into my lungs. I couldn't take deep breaths, but I could breathe. It hurt so bad to take a breath and it made me incredibly mad. I would force myself to sit up and I would force myself to walk from the couch to the bathroom.

Once a day I forced myself down the stairs whenever I woke up. Then late into the night I forced myself back up those stairs to go back to bed. I made myself walk to the kitchen to get myself something to drink.

On the worst night I woke up alone on the couch and I just couldn't take it anymore. I went into the kitchen, boiled water, and jazzed up a jar of pasta sauce. I had no idea what time it was, but I knew it was late and no one was bothering to cook dinner.

I was mad at my family, I was mad at myself, and I was especially mad at the state of the world. I'm not sure the how's or the why's on the state of the world. My only guess is that I was listening to the news while I slept on the couch. I put that dinner together and sat my butt back on the couch and the flood gates opened.

I know how cliché that sounds, but it is exactly what happened. Not knowing what day it was, all the ridiculousness of the past two years, all my personal failures, and my inability to catch my breath and stop the tears was entirely too much.

I had finally cracked. My daughter found me sobbing and trying to catch my breath. She was going to cook after all.

I woke up to a scary conversation.

"She needs to go to the hospital now."

"I don't care what she says, she can't breathe."

Oh hell no. One thing I was certain of is that the people who were dying were going to the hospital. Nope, not going to happen. On a good day I hate doctors on a bad day, I do not trust them. I had never been sick or in an emergency in my entire life where a doctor was able to help.

Most of the time doctors made it worse. I had paid attention enough to the 'news' to know that doctors had no idea what they were doing. I had to make my stand.

"I'll go to the doctor in the morning." Yeah, I know,

I'm tough. In my defense I was sick. I didn't have the strength to argue. Just between you and me, I was ready to take whatever it was they gave the former president. Whatever it did to me in twenty years was not my concern. I was ready to breathe.

The next day at whatever time I managed to wake up and shower unassisted, my daughter had already made me an appointment. There was a new variant and a not so new variant. One caused less issues than the other which meant my daughter was able to go in with me. I didn't understand it either, I was just glad to have someone with me.

I was ushered into a room with my kid and told to wait. The nurse came in and gave me a COVID test and two different flu tests. She saw me gasping for air and told me to take my mask down so I could breathe. That made medical sense to everyone in the room.

I mean they were masked, why make me suffocate? She left, came back, and yup, I was positive. "The doctor will be in shortly."

Meanwhile we are left in the hottest doctor's office I had ever been in. I had to take off my sweatshirt. My daughter looked over at the thermostat and it sat at a solid seventy-eight degrees. Viruses thrive in hot places, everyone knows that. It seemed very off to me but being off made me be very aware of my surroundings and everything going on.

In my mind, all the sleep had prepared me for this moment. Have you ever watched a scary movie and all of a sudden the heroine figures out who the murder is? That was me sitting in the doctor's office. The doctor came rushing through the door in her paper gown, mask, and shield, takes one look at me and says, "Put on your mask!"

THE CHAOS OF COVID

Never mind that the nurse said to take it off. The doctor was short with me and more than a little mean. She basically just told me to go to the emergency room.

Exiting the building was an experience. We were sent down this narrow hallway with chairs full of patients on each side. Apparently, this is the section people sat while waiting for their COVID tests to come back. The waiting room was large, open, and quite spacious without a soul in it.

The COVID testers were put in a tiny hallway and me, the COVID positive patient, was sent to walk between them. The only thing between all those people and my COVID germs was our thin paper masks. I did the only thing I could, I held my breath as we walked through the corridor. I may live to be hundred and ten years old and I will never understand the logic of that hallway situation.

The hospital was the craziest place with the weirdest rules my little conspiracy brain could wrap my head around. No one was allowed in with me. I did not like that at all, but rules are rules. They asked if I could walk. I am positive I said yes. Maybe my daughter said no or maybe I just looked that bad.

Some lady came rushing up with the world's most uncomfortable steel contraption disguised as a wheelchair and ran right over my toes, all five of them. Once I could no longer walk, the chair was nice. I went to triage to get my vitals and another COVID test. Apparently the first test did not count.

Two COVID tests still gets to me. There was a shortage of tests at that time in Atlanta and there I was getting two. You know what though, there was still the factor of the fifty percent fail rate, hmm. Positive again. I was winning the COVID lottery! My pulse was fast, blood pressure low, my oxygen was low, and they were concerned.

"You go to the top of the list."

Then out to the waiting room I went. This is where I start coming to my senses. I might have been getting better or it was just the amount of air I was getting from prolonged sitting up. My brain was clearing by the minute, and I was taking everything in. The waiting room could probably hold two hundred people comfortably.

It was quite empty with maybe fifteen people in there. Everyone was spaced out except for me and the lady they wheeled me within six feet of. The coffee table had a little note about social distancing and how they took pride in how clean things were.

Eventually the lady got called back and another lady came in and sat in her exact seat. No one had come over and wiped down that seat. I chuckled or tried to chuckle. I started watching the door. It was a pandemic, surely there were going to be a hundred people in the waiting room before long.

I just pictured us all breathing on each other spreading our variants around like an STD. Nope. I saw a guy with a broken leg come in and I saw an old man. The guy with the broken leg was put into one of the wheelchair things that I saw a lady come out of ten minutes prior. No one wiped that chair out first.

I was starting to have real concerns about that hospital. Up at the nurses' station no one had a mask on. If a patient came up, they pulled their masks up but if no one was around those masks rocked the chins. They were not afraid of each other, just of us and I did not blame them at all.

Eventually they came to get me. They wheeled me into a low-pressure room and left me there for a what seemed like forever. I asked to use the restroom when someone finally showed up and they directed me to walk down the hallway about two hundred feet away. They said if I had any issues to pull the emergency lever.

I don't know what I was supposed to do if I had an issue before I got to the bathroom. Surprisingly I safely made it there and back. Then it was time to fill out the paperwork. This is when I realized I had forgotten my glasses and I couldn't see a thing. I asked for a patient advocate but because of COVID there wasn't one.

I made a little joke about nothing I signed being legal if I couldn't see it and the nurse nervously laughed. Getting my insurance card out was fun. I couldn't see and she wasn't legally allowed to get it for me. We played a little game of me pulling out every card in my wallet one by one until I got the right one. Good times. I went to x-ray, came back, and took a nice long nap until the doctor finally showed up.

Dr. Bollywood had a purple shirt and fabulous hair. He walked in with the sureness of a god. "You have a terrible cough."

"I haven't coughed at all."

"You have a terrible cough. You have COVID pneumonia," he tossed his feathered hair back like an eighties rock star.

"I'll give you pneumonia and COVID."

He sent me home with a cough suppressant and told me to take Tylenol. I was not impressed.

I think I am one of those people who thrives on chaos and anger. I complained all the way home. I recounted my story to everyone who would listen. I'm pretty sure they sent me home to die, but I wasn't going to die of COVID.

I was too mad to die. Every day I got stronger. It took a month before I could get out of the house on my own. I still couldn't get a deep breath, but I was negative, and I was over it.

Several weeks later I sat on my friend's living room floor and caught up with life for hours and hours. We hung out and I confessed that I was jonesing for a drag of her cigarette. Crazy, I couldn't breathe, but that menthol smelled like heaven. I did the stupidest thing I have ever done in my entire life.

I took a drag off her cigarette and inhaled it deep into my lungs. Guess what happened. I took a deep breath, and another, and another, and I've been breathing just fine since. I am not a doctor. I am a conspiracy theorist. I do not recommend anyone be as stupid as I was. Inhaling smoke into your lungs is bad for your health. I am simply explaining what happened to me.

Don't even think about doing it. Smoking while recovering from pneumonia shows a lack of cognitive ability. The lack of oxygen most certainly robbed me of IQ points. There was talk about banning menthol cigarettes though. I'm sure that's just my conspiracy brain thinking out loud. This is my story of how I didn't have COVID three times, but I did have it once.

About the Author
Michelle Angone

Michelle Angone is an internationally published author. She has written on women's issues in UK's "Riot Angel" magazine as well as several small print zines using short fiction, poetry, and essay.

A reluctant academic, she has majored in just about everything from nursing to philosophy. What she lacks in diploma she makes up for with certificates and initiations. She is a priestess of several paths and a student of the mysteries.

Currently, she is a homeschool mom, teaching paganism to children whose families fall outside the typical homeschool norm. As a lover of the arts, Michelle has been a lifelong vocalist, occasional aspiring performer, and a former children's choir instructor.

She enjoys speculating on the world around her, be it the seen or unseen. Her curiosity tends to cost her many hours of endless research into the occult and conspiracy theories, and wherever the two collide.

This pastime rewards her with lots of aha moments and even more laughs. Michelle lives in North Georgia with her husband of thirty years, her children, an acquired grand dog, and her baby cat. A herd of deer rely on the Nana and Bog Witch for their morning and evening meals.

Once a day, a group of juvenile delinquent crows demand corn tortillas from her in exchange for their silence and her sanity. Although a bit outspoken and more than a little bit opinionated, Michelle enjoys a quiet life in her witchy cottage in the woods.

Chapter 10

Mask it Up Buttercup

By Laura Greene

The rain poured down. Not the gentle kind that taps at a window. The bucket emptying, sewer filling, flash flooding, gully washer type of rain. Freezing cold. I stood ankle deep in the rising water.

My jeans became saturation barometers as the thirsty denim greedily sucked the water up my legs inch by uncomfortable inch. Every step made more complicated by my sneaker's newly discovered ability to float. As if the shoe desired to come off of my foot and join the rest of the detritus merrily swirling towards to storm drain.

I've no idea how far the asphalt parking lot actually is from the building but it felt like acres.

It had been raining steadily since I arrived at my Grandma's house earlier that day.

"It's raining," said my Grandma.

"I know it is, but we have to go to the doctor."

"Dr Harmondy," she asked.

"Yup," I said, herding her towards the back door.

She's completely covered foot to hair in old lady rain gear. Snow boots, the only non-sandal, non-sneaker footwear I was able to get onto her uncooperative feet. Elastic waist jeans with the sewn on patch pockets, short sleeve top (because having to remove her shirt for the customary blood pressure reading is a big to-do), and a stained cardigan sweater.

She also wore an early 90's winter coat fuchsia and teal, and oversized plastic rain bonnet—the kind with a built-in bill that extends far out over the forehead and ties underneath her chin. It resembles an incredibly posh bread bag.

Getting out the back door of her house involves a multistep process. Actually, everything involving my Grandma is a multistep process but I digress. First I stand in front of her walker outside of the wooden door holding open the storm door with my body. She then holds onto the doorframe and the door knob, turns herself around and steps down backwards one foot at a time.

Next comes the tricky part, getting her to turn back around facing forwards and not continuing to walk backwards into the walker. The distance from the doorway + granny + walker places me underneath the gutter which, while not being clogged, still manages to dump leafy torrents over its side and onto my head.

I had an umbrella in one hand but the storm door opening does not allow for holding it upright but jutted out to the side.

Feet finally on the ground, and facing the correct direction, my Grandma and her walker began to move forward. Between her single car garage and the side of the house is a four foot covered walkway. We reached the end of this walkway and again, stop.

"It's raining," said my Grandma.

"I know it is, but we have to go to the doctor."

"Dr Harmondy," she asked.

"Yes," I shouted to be heard over the rain.

"Well, good God." She marches forward.

Walker. step. Walker. Step. Walker. Step. Turns out that to be a decent human being and keep the umbrella over the plastic bonneted head of the nonagenarian you must extend your one arm fully forward. This leaves you, the umbrella holder, fully exposed to the rain.

Then, with my grandma relishing this situation, the edge of the umbrella lines up with my face— so thwarted from falling to the ground, the raindrops slide down the umbrella and joyously land on my glasses, in my eyes, in my hair, and somehow bypass both my coat and top to travel down my neck.

Reaching the end of the five foot distance to the car comes another tricky maneuver—getting into the vehicle. My Grandma lets go of the walker, and opens the car door, thus leaving her nothing whatsoever to stabilize herself.

With the car door open and the rain helpfully now coming in sideways to dampen the interior, I use the non-umbrella hand to pull the walker to the side and keep the umbrella as best I can over the car door opening.

The free hand then attempts to hold tightly to my Grandma's arm, who intentionally free falls backwards into the passenger seat. Once in, she slides her feet around to the footwell and slams the car door. This is the only way my Grandma knows how to close any door.

The classic slam.

It probably dates back to a time when car doors were heavy steel affairs. Thankfully, this time my person and clothing had all cleared the space sufficiently and nothing was caught.

To close the walker requires two hands: one to push in the lever and the other to swing in the side. Bending at the waist I am able to accomplish collapsing the right-hand side of the walker without letting go of the umbrella. The left-hand side, always the more stubborn of the two, refuses my awkward grip.

I carry the half-folded walker to the back of the car, open the hatch, set in the umbrella, finish folding the walker, umbrella out, walker in, hatch shut. Now, umbrella down and self into car.

"I don't have my purse," said my Grandma before my car door is even shut.

"It's in the back seat," I said. Because of the rain I had placed both her purse, my purse, and the indispensable geriatric back pack (basically a diaper bag) in a pile behind the passenger seat.

"No it isn't," She argued. She kept looking only into the back seat visible behind the driver's side.

"It is," I assured her as I put my own seatbelt on, "It's behind you."

"Cause I don't see it." She continued looking at exactly the same part of the back seat.

I reach back around, grab the purse, bringing it up and setting it in the wet footwell. Satisfied, she began to fasten her seat belt. I backed out of the driveway.

My grandparent's driveway is a special tribute to the effective design of retaining walls and concrete. At some point in the 1970's (maybe?) the city or the county or the port authority or whomever came through with imminent domain over half of the front lawn of the house to widen the street.

The amputated lawn thus became three feet of sod surrounded by the front walk and concrete retaining walls four feet high. Thus the driveway began approximately one car length of gravel and then changed to concrete and steeply sloped down the remaining few feet into the street.

A standard size pickup truck cannot back down this driveway without scraping. So while avoiding the erosion drop off on the left side, and the aforementioned concrete wall on the right I backed into the street which Monday through Friday serves as the main entrance and exit to a semi-Truck filling depot. It is the middle of a weekday.

I heard the clicking of the metal seatbelt buckle against the receptacle. Once. Twice. Three times. I generally waited until she got frustrated with it. She brought her hand up, adjusted the belt, pulled it way out in front to create more room. The reality was her hands didn't have the strength to snap the buckle.

Or maybe it was the coordination. The truck traffic provided a break. We did the backing up while turning the wheels maneuver that got us safely across the wide lanes, over the median, and facing the correct direction. Simultaneously I reached out and snapped her seat belt buckle home. It made a satisfying sound.

"Oh!" My Grandma makes an exasperated, but smiling gesture as she usually does over the seatbelt. As if to say, "Can you believe that?"

At this juncture—yes. Yes, I can believe it.

Less than half a block from the house is a stop light. It's red. It's always red unless there's a truck needing to exit. We began to wait for the traffic light. She looked down into the footwell for her purse. Presumably she saw it because she settled back. She immediately looked in the footwell again,

"Where's my cane," she asked.

"We don't have it," I replied.

"What?"

She didn't hear me. I stopped concentrating on the red traffic light and turned to face her repeating, "We don't have it."

"Oh hell. Well, we'd better go back for it," she said.

"We have the walker," I explained.

"The walker?" She looked confused, "But I use a cane."

"Today we brought the walker."

My Father's funeral had taken place about three years ago and was repeatedly interrupted first by a loud voice, "I can't find my cane!"

Followed by a series of shh-ing noises from people seated around my Grandma. Then an equally loud stage whisper, "I can't find my cane."

My uncle seated beside her reached down, picked up the cane, handed it to her, and she immediately set it down in the exact spot it came from. In hindsight I might have saved myself some arguments if I had continued keeping the cane in the car and then just not using it.

But at that moment the cane was back at her house hidden inside the recesses of a closet. The cane had to be hidden so she couldn't decide to use it instead of her walker. I also had to hide all the Ensure to prevent her from drinking it all in one day.

The stop light turned green. The doctor's appointment was originally scheduled for early in March of 2020. The appointment was a routine physical. My Grandma was a ninety-eight-year-old woman with appointments every six months. Due to the emerging Corona Virus I hesitated to take her anywhere.

First, the appointment was pushed back a couple of weeks. Then I pushed it back a few more. Then my Grandma's sister Rose, aged ninety-five died of Covid. Rose lived out of state so the two sisters had not had recent contact. There would be no funeral services because of the lockdown.

The priest at Rose's parish had a recording of the funeral on Facebook so that loved ones could watch. I suppose for some families this might have been comforting. Personally, I think my great aunt would have been beyond appalled that her last day at mass was broadcast on social media.

I'm not sure she knew what social media was. I did not know how my Grandma would take the news of her sister's passing. I didn't know if she would even remember it. I agonized over telling her the sad news. Finally I told her earlier that morning. She said, "I'm the only one left now."

This is why I was taking her to the doctor's in the pouring rain. I thought having something to do—even something such as a doctor's appointment might help her cope with this most recent death. I learned later that in terms of Covid my keeping the appointment at this time was neither here nor there.

The odds of someone ninety-eight dying of Covid were greater than 60% however, her odds of dying from literally any other cause was still significantly greater. Dr Harmondy was a tall, kind, balding man of seventy. He had attended Grade School and High School with my father.

Apparently, my father didn't like the man fifty-two years ago and my grandma reminded me of this fact every single visit. Even though he had been her primary care physician for over forty years. She remembered my Dad had not cared for him. She never entertained any thought of changing doctors.

The windshield wipers on the highest setting didn't help visibility, but the route was familiar enough I hoped that wouldn't matter. I was scared. I didn't want to be taking my Grandma out of the house at all let alone to the doctor since presumably that was where sick people went.

I had been assured by the receptionist that anyone with Covid symptoms wasn't allowed to come into the office. She may have meant this fact to be reassuring. This fact was not comforting. The idea that should my grandmother get Covid she then wouldn't be allowed in to see her doctor… This unsettling thought had to take its place in the queue of more immediate unsettling thoughts.

I had begun a search for at-home help for my grandma in 2018. Finding a caregiver was an arduous process for which I was completely unprepared. She was ninety-six years old at that time. So it might have occurred to me she would need assistance but it had not. And I don't know why it had not.

I encountered disappearing caregivers who would show up for orientation and then never come back. I encountered well intentioned caregivers who would call me for every single small matter thus, not really helping alleviate the burden of caring.

I encountered women fired by the agency. This last one happened frequently. This process stressed me out significantly more than my grandma who never remembered who the caregivers were anyway. I finally found an angel of a woman named Michelle. She stayed with us through an incredibly rude management situation at the agency.

Michelle had been exposed to Covid at another patient's house and then she too could not help with my Grandma. This is one reason I ended up transporting my Grandma to the doctor's in the pouring rain alone.

Covid put a freeze on all non-emergency nursing home placements. This meant that even if I somehow managed to find a memory care facility we could afford—they are expensive as hell—she would not be allowed in. I was therefore stuck with minimal help from at home caregivers. The home health agency's Covid policy was the caregiver had to test negative before being allowed to return to work.

Getting a Covid test at this time took at least a week in a best case scenario. This was not the best case scenario. The agency sent all their employees to a specific testing site at a drug store in another town. The results could be two weeks away.

I carefully pulled my car into the pot-holed parking lot of the primary care physician's office. I parked as close to the main doors as was possible. This wasn't all that close given where the wheel-chair-entrance was located. This was the moment I realized the only ally I had counted on being there was not.

The valet parking service was discontinued. Parking valets were not considered essential workers. I knew the valet. There was only one for this clinic. His name was Josh. He wore a stocking cap with a Batman emblem on it. Tall, with a wife and two kids, he was always opening the door and helping. Because of Covid I had no caregiver. Because of Covid I had no valet. Because of Covid I had no help.

I put on the car's hazard lights. I got out the cloth face masks I had made and was so proud of. I tied my grandma's on first. Leaning over I had to tie first the bottom ties around her neck, and then the pulled up the top set.

The fabric was navy blue with St. Louis Cardinals baseball emblems on it. I'd sewn hundreds of masks for my friends and my community. All ties because there was no elastic in the craft stores. I thought my Grandma would love her favorite baseball team but if she noticed the pattern at all, she never said.

Looking back at her face I had managed to pull the mouth covering piece up over her eyes like a blindfold. She just sat still unable to see, glasses up on her forehead. I readjusted it. I then put my own face mask on. She then started to open her car door.

"Wait for me," I yelled.

She swung her feet around.

Hurriedly, I pulled my own mask down off my face and got her attention.

"Wait for me, please."

THE CHAOS OF COVID

Almost all dialogue with my Grandmother is shouted. She has extreme bilateral hearing loss. To be able to understand people at all she became quite adept at lip reading. Or she could lipread before Covid. The face masks were not conducive to this situation.

Because she couldn't understand anyone when they had a face mask on, she assumed that they, in turn, couldn't understand her. She would just point at her covered mouth or would try to take it off to speak. Neither was useful.

Getting out of the car I grabbed first the umbrella, then the walker. Thankfully, the contraption unfolds with one hand. My grandma had the car door open and was struggling to get up out of the seat in the few seconds it took me to get from the rear hatch to the passenger door.

I swallowed down my irritation. My mind continually narrated my situation going straight through self-pity and out the other side into self-deprecation and back the other way.

Leaving my unlocked car, flashers on at the curb, I'm able to take her inside the first part of the building. There's a pre-waiting room with vintage vinyl seating and an equally vintage pair of vending machines. With a series of shouted commands and gestures I'm able to explain sitting and waiting for me to get back.

My jeans water level is now past my knees. The only open parking space is not in the lot attached to the building, but across a narrow road to an overflow lot. I didn't remember there typically being a stream to wade through, but the day proved full of surprises.

I could've cried I guess. I didn't have the time to cry. It's a pandemic. Everyone is stressed. Everyone is suffering. There's literally no rest for the weary and no sense complaining because everyone has their own version of this equal opportunity hell.

Reaching the double sliding doors of the entrance I panted in my facemask, out of breath. I was wet. I was cold. To my surprise, my grandma was exactly where I'd left her. An older couple stood in front of her asking if she was okay.

"She's with me," I explained.

"Who are you?" My grandma asked the couple.

Apparently this was the first she had spoken to them. Having taken in the half-drowned woman and the elderly lady they looked pityingly at me.

"I'm just taking care of a nonagenarian in the middle of a pandemic in the middle of a thunderstorm," I said laughing.

"Lord have mercy," said the older women as they left.

On us all I thought. On. Us. All.

Special Dedications by the author, Laura Greene (Bio on Page 200):

In memory of Sophie Wendel 12-15-21 to 02-01-21, and Jean Draper 02-11-32 to 06-07-22 may my Grandmothers by biology and by spirit rest peacefully and be with us from the other side.

Dedicated to David Mayberry. You've been a rock throughout my hospice adventure with my Grandma. Thank You for taking care of our fur family while I traveled to and fro for so long. I love you and am very excited for our future together.

Dedicated to Aahara—especially Carley Mattimore, and John Malan for teaching me (or attempting to teach me) to walk between the worlds.

Dedicated to Ruth Souther for teaching me what the worlds we walk between are, thank you Spirit Mama.

Dedicated to PJ & Katie for your unwavering support and friendship throughout the adventure portrayed in the story as well as all the many adventures that have come after. I genuinely hope our paths remain together for years to come. See you next game!

This is on everyone.

Chapter 11

Fourever Hopeful:
A Poem About Feeling Aimlessly Angry
(For All the Good That Does)

By Laura Greene

Have you ever been angry? Angry at a person, at people, at a concept, at the world? Sometimes it grows, anger, until it tints and distorts everything you see, everything you feel, everything you believe.

Then sometimes it does something unexpected—it fades. Writing this poem began from shock and anger. Anger at this collection specifically as we were warned all viewpoints would be expressed. It felt socially irresponsible to be written up in the same work as someone anti-mask or anti-vac.

It felt gross. It felt the opposite of integrity. It brought up a lot of feelings. Then came an explanation about how it wasn't exactly this and wasn't exactly that. The anti-mask viewpoint had such a good reason, and didn't that make it ok? I'm not sure.

I've pondered this question for weeks now. Does the reasoning behind someone's anti-mask, anti-vac choice make it valid? Is there a Venn diagram where personal choices and social responsibility meet? What would this overlap be called if it exists?

My feelings remain strong that every person not getting the vaccine contributes to a larger problem. A body of millions creating the perfect breeding ground for a new viral variant threat. A collective of people blatantly saying to the world: *you are not my concern.*

I don't know that in any other situation I'd be inclined to say that someone's reasoning doesn't matter. That personal choice is no longer relevant. This is dangerous ground ethically, yet here I am wanting to say it.

Your reasons are not relevant. You are contributing to the problem.

This is not based on scientific data. This is my feelings born out of my own exceedingly limited knowledge of virology and fear. My fear would have every single person vaccinated to try to fight back a virus. I'm a fan of survival horror.

It's humanity versus a virus and we will prevail. But this is real life, not survival horror. In the world not depicted on television there's this huge indifferent mass of humanity that cannot be moved to change their minds about vaccines, or masking, or (and this is an unfair assumption) anything.

Nothing during the time of Covid went as I was expecting it to. But did things always turn out how I expected them to before Covid? Of course not. So why now should it be surprising that life both zigs and zags and at times loops the loop just when we're physically prepared for a straight away?

I've two examples. First, the day before yesterday I went to the grocery store to buy boneless skinless chicken breasts. In my household this is a typical menu item. The warehouse store I typically buy them at was out. The discount grocer was out.

The local market had two packs in excess of $15 which were prices I was unwilling to pay. The big box store was having a computer issue and all the card readers were down for the evening—I was therefore unable to check if they had chicken since I lacked the cash necessary for the purchase.

This is what grocery shopping has become. Things never previously scarce are frequently sold out and previously economical items no longer are affordable. This is the year 2022. This is supposedly two years after ground zero for Covid.

Secondly, writing this poem for this book did not go as expected. (Thank you reader's for your patience with this meta-example.) I began writing feeling angry, stayed angry, passed through anger, circled back, got confused, wanted to quit, got depressed, felt resigned, became indifferent, and wound up somewhere amidst all these feelings like a forgotten thumb tack on an explanatory bulletin board.

My feelings zigged when I realized all viewpoints would be represented in this book, and then just when I was coming to process these feelings they zagged by my then being asked to write an introduction to this poem.

Why? I thought poems didn't have introductions. They need no explanations. They're art. Poems should be solidly in the realm of expletives not exposition. My expectations were to smack the hypothetical reader right in the face with a poem. Wham! Poem.

Here is how I feel and I offer you no explanation let alone several paragraphs of analysis to the wherefores and whys. Doesn't this make the situation confusing? Less clear? Emotionally yucky? Doesn't this process sound a lot like a Covid story?

Yup. They're unavoidable. Everyone, everywhere is living a version of a story within a story within a pandemic on a backdrop of historical political unrest and generalized global upheaval. I just wrote a paragraph on the frustrations of buying chicken while there's a war going on in the Ukraine.

I wrote a blog about housecleaning while thousands were actively dying in the ICU from Covid-19. A person can't stay long in this existential realm.

Was writing this poem cathartic? My firm definitive response is: kind of. While on one level unsatisfying this wishy washy answer is refreshingly honest. We inhabit a new world of kind of, almost, sort of, and gray.

It is murky. Maybe the market has chicken this week maybe it doesn't. Maybe this is seasonal allergies or maybe I'm sick. Ever present the fear of getting, or more frequently getting again the virus whose namesake this entire work was meant to memorialize.

This situation is not entirely new. There have always been yayhoos and fringe beliefs mucking up all sorts of legislation and writing collaboratives. Somehow though the volume feels louder.

No longer are there conspiratorial murmurs but dedicated conspiratorial major news networks. The one fact that is not debatable and is a cliche because it so true is this one: we are all in this together. For better or worse. One planet. One tribe. One stew (possibly without chicken.)

Fourever Hopeful

Two plus two equals four.

Two plus two equals five.

Two plus two equals four.
Surely they'll realize their mistake in a minute.

Two plus two equals five.
Two plus two equals five.

Two plus two equals four.
Here, let me show you:
Four tires on a car: one, two, three, four.
Four paws on a dog: one, two, three, four.

Two plus two equals five.
Everyone knows a car has a spare tire, five!
I don't see how that's relevant anyway.
I once saw a dog with three legs, and it lived.

Two plus two equals four.
We used to live in a world where facts mattered.
Where ignorance was corrected.
Where not knowing something meant a chance to learn.

Two plus two equals five.
The facts are being twisted to suit the elite.

History has been white washed to hide the truth.
Fake news. Five. Fake news.

Two plus two equals four.
Facts are being ignored to suit the ignorant.
History is not being consulted.
Just google two plus two. Please.

Two plus two equals five.
There is no truth but that inside oneself.
I will not be led as a sheep to the shearing.
Preach the gospel of five or die trying.

Two plus two equals four.
But shearing doesn't harm the sheep…
I'm not even sure what you're saying?
Truth can, in fact, be factual.

Two plus two equals five.
Big pharma wants us to be sheared.
Without wool we die naked and afraid.
I will die with my coat intact.

Two plus two equals four.
No one need die at all; the science is sound.
Just please count with me:
One. Two. Three. Four.

Two plus two equals five.
You know who counts? Sheep.
I will never be a sheep.
I will die free.

THE CHAOS OF COVID

Two plus two equals four.
This seems very dramatic for a simple equation.
Maybe we should just let them be?
Can fours live in a world with fives?

Two plus two equals five.
I will never wear a mask.
I will not vaccinate my children.
My feelings are valid.

Two plus two equals four.
Whoa Whoa whoa, now hang on—
your children?
You're sacrificing your children now for the sake of
five?!

Two plus two equals five.
You can't tell me what to do.
They're my children, my belongings.
My body, my rules.

Two plus two equals four.
But there's this virus that really unites humanity.
We want the fives to be safe.
We want the five's children to be healthy.

Five.
How dare you interfere with my children.
I will never wear a mask.
I will never get the vaccine.

Two plus two equals four.
That is… your choice….
But your children…
shouldn't they—

Two plus two equals five.
Five. Five.
Feelings are valid. Five.
It's the ultimate test of our faith in five.

Four.
I just think we've lost the plot here
faith doesn't even enter in,
I mean I can show you the data—

Five is all that matters.
All fives matter.
How dare you call us ignorant.
How dare you judge us, this country is free.

Four.
Just four.
One, two, three, four.
Right?

Two plus two equals five.
We will take this country back in the name of five.
Make five great again!
Five score and seven years ago our fathers…

Two plus two equals four.

THE CHAOS OF COVID

Four score. Not five.
Please just look it up.
Here's the link—just read anything.

Two plus two equals five.
The vaccine puts a microchip into the bloodstream.
The masks keep us silent about five.
The virus is a conspiracy.

Two plus two equals four.
I don't even know where to begin.
What if I chose to believe six?
What if six was how I felt?

Two plus two equals five.
There's no such thing as six.
No one believes in six.
I'd murder someone who believed six.

Two plus two (does in fact) equal four.
But doesn't six have the same rights as five?
I mean it isn't about rights,
only facts but just for the sake of argument.

Two plus two always has been five.
They hide their five under a bushel.
God created man and woman for five.
Not six. Same six marriages are an abomination.

Two plus two equals four.
There's a lot of erroneous information here.
Let's just be clear.

Wear a mask, it makes us all safer.

Two plus two equals five.
My neighbor's daughter's aunt died of cancer.
She wore a mask.
That's what mask wearing gets people, death.

Two plus two equals four.
I'm very sorry about the aunt.
Cancer isn't a virus.
This conversation is about a virus, not cancer.

Two plus two equals five forever and ever amen.
The fours would have you believe this is about a virus.
There is no virus.
There is no four.

Four.
There is a virus.
There is four.
There is verifiable proof of vaccine effectiveness.

Two plus two equals five.
Go within and find your five.
Vote five, stay alive.
Never be told what to do.

Two plus two equals four.
You know what, I'm done.
I don't even want to be associated in anyway with fives.
The Karens, the Yayhoos, the ridiculous.
Two plus two equals five.

THE CHAOS OF COVID

This is how I feel, and it is valid.
Therefore, it is fact.
You cannot tell me how I feel.

Two plus two equals four.
To the children: Not all of us are fives.
Some of us with love and compassion know the truth.

One. Two. Three. Four.
Two plus two equals five.
Right here, right now is a great time to be five.
We will not wear masks.
We will face the future unafraid.

Four.
It's just about love and holding space.
Vaccines save lives.
Mask wearing helps the entire situation.

Five is and was and always will be…
I can't breathe.
I can't breathe…
Four, help, please.

One. Two. Three. Four. Five…
Breath. Breath.
One. Two. Three. Four. Five….
Breath. Breath.

Though may I walk in the valley in the shadow of five…
Here I am to testify to five.
Five saves lives.

I had faith in five and though I got very sick I didn't die.

Two plus two equals four.
I literally just saved your life with my science.
My ventilator.
My vaccine.

Praise be to the faith in five.
Let us sing:
Two plus two is five.
Five is our everything.

Four.
Unbelievable.

Five.
The fours have no faith.
Don't let them take yours away.
Five and five and five.

Two plus two equals four.
To our children: We fought the good fight.
We stand with the truth.
And the truth never waivers.

Two plus two equals five.
We live in a world where the feelings about a situation
become the situation itself.
As it should be.

Two plus two equals four.
Study.

THE CHAOS OF COVID

Learn.
Vaccines Save lives.

Two plus two equals five.
Don't believe the hype!
Don't believe the scientists.
Don't believe anything other than five!

Two plus two equals four.
Believe.
In spite of everything.
It's all going to be ok.

When I was initially asked the question, *What is your Covid story?* my answer was, *I don't have one.* My personal Covid experiences felt pedestrian. In March of 2020 I worked like crazy listing items in my online store. I hoped for a brief quarantine because bored people stuck at home—shop.

As a very small online reseller I wanted my piece of this once-in-a-lifetime pie. Then the quarantine happened and my boyfriend was sent home from work. The nature of his job does not lend itself to work from home, and thus I drafted him into my frenzy.

We worked constantly at online sales until a short time later when everyone was asked to wear a face mask. The stores had no masks. I can sew. I went from working fifteen hour days for my own financial gain—to sewing all day, every day for my community.

I used my own fabric stash. I watched YouTube videos on sewing face masks. I coordinated thread. I taught my boyfriend how to iron. I sewed, and sewed, and sewed.

When the stores very quickly ran out of elastic I learned to sew fabric ties. I sewed masks for everyone: friends, neighbors, the mail lady, and two local shops. I sewed hundreds of masks.

The only person I knew who died from Covid was one of the two shop owners selling my masks. When I made her rather large order it had taken a considerable amount of work and she had a rack already full of cheap single layer masks.

At a time when my orders were still in the dozens I found this rude. I later regretted my response. She chose not to wear a mask because it made it hard for her to breathe. This was our last conversation. Her choice to not mask was startling because this was a time before anti-mask or anti-vac garnered so much attention. There was no vaccine yet and the face mask resistance seemed more comical than dangerous.

When I learned this book may well represent someone of a differing opinion than myself I was (as has already been thoroughly covered) angry. Before I set about writing however I did what I frequently do when disappointed and angry: I called my best friend Christina.

I explained to her I had been excited to be a part of a Covid collaborative book but then it was revealed they were letting in *the Karens*. Christina introduced me to the all-encompassing term: yayhoos.

We talked at length about my fears surrounding this. How could anybody in good conscious publish with such ignorant yayhoos expressing their opinion as fact? And facts as fictitious?

She explained it me this way: "It used to be two plus two equals four. And someone would say, 'two plus two equals five' and we'd say, 'oh, you're mistaken—here let me show you...'

"And that'd be the end of it. Ignorance used to be cured by education. After all, the reality is, we're all ignorant in some subjects. It wasn't a bad thing—ignorance. It's become a curse word or terrible insult calling someone ignorant.

"While it is true no one likes to be ignorant now it's as if there's no such thing. You're not ignorant, you just have a different opinion. If you want to believe two plus two equals five then not only is that supposed to be valid but is supposed to be treated with equal respect to the truth. It no longer matters that it isn't true."

Then she said these most brilliant of words:

"Can you submit two stories?"

"I think so," I said, "Why?"

"Because this—this whole discussion we've been having. This *is* a Covid story."

She's right. She's usually right. Out of our conversation, but also out of my own fears, prejudices, insecurity, pain, and undying resilience and resignation came the above poem.

Throughout its creation I had but one thought: When the daughters of all of us read this in years to come—please, please know we went down fighting. In August of 2019 a plaque was dedicated to the first death of a glacier. The plaque reads:

Ok (Okjökull) is the first Icelandic glacier to lose its status as a glacier. In the next 200 years all our glaciers are expected to follow the same path. This monument is to acknowledge that we know what is happening and what needs to be done. Only you know if we did it.

This same spirit moves me to assure the future of…
something. One angry poem from the Midwest to reassure
future generations we saw the multitudes of unvaccinated
and wrote about it? In essence, yes.

Have you tried to see the yayhoos' points of view? Not
really. It isn't entirely accurate to say I don't care, but
Covid has proven especially good at finding the sweet spot
over and over again of lethality and communicability.

The danger is all the millions of unvaccinated persons
have their own story. They each have their own arsenal of
personal reasons for not *taking the jab*. The jab. The
lifesaving, world restoring, first line of defense was being
sabotaged and reduced to one trite nickname. There is an
irony here, likely only appreciated in hindsight, of not
understanding one's place in the collective—following a
time where slogans such as, *we're all in this together*
permeated.

I feel a curious void sensation what to do with them…
to look into the face of someone literally deciding they
were singlehandedly more important than…everyone?

They don't see it this way I'm sure. But it is the truth.
They're perpetuating a problem knowingly and willfully.
And they want me to understand their point of view.

No, I just don't.

About the Author
Laura Greene

Laura Greene is unmistakably a midwestern aspiring writer, a dedicated reseller of goods, and occasionally an exasperated pet owner.

Dedicated always to Christina (Sissa) & her family—Jay, Brooklyn, Jamison, Harrison, & Landyn. May this story's negativity be comedically untrue in the future and may we still be friends to laugh at it over coffee.

Dedicated to Caroline for her loyal friendship, ever present ear, and special thanks for editing. Don't let the yayhoos or the yahoos bring you down.

I'm so angry.

Chapter 12

Online Anywhere:
Teaching and Learning
Happens Where I Am

By Pam Daniel

The world changed, in so many ways, as COVID took over our lives. We started communicating online, and teachers started to teach and learn online. I have been a college instructor since 1987. I was ready, and eager, to teach online when the need arose in Spring 2019.

Have you taken an online course? Perhaps graphic design, accounting, or a public speaking class? Were you happy about having that option to learn something new? Was the topic exciting or frustrating? Where were you actually sitting down at your computer to participate in the lessons?

Although perhaps you used a tablet or cell phone to

read, and listen, and do. It does, and it doesn't, matter how you were presented with the concepts and ideas; What's really important is how it made you feel about learning, and what you remember.

Because of Covid, our collective need to use technology as a way to communicate was heaved forward all at once. Students at all levels needed to continue their learning, and teachers were forced to figure out how to make that happen. It has been challenging and devastating for many people, it has been a miraculous godsend for others.

On my life's journey, I've witnessed astounding technological changes in the way people communicate. Covid gave me opportunities I have been working toward as a teacher and enabled me to achieve my professional goals.

As an innately curious person, I love to learn new things. And there is something to learn everywhere I find myself, in every experience. Finding that gem is easier if I push myself to be in the moment. And once identified, I enjoy sharing what I learned with other people.

My joy of learning led me to become a teacher. And naturally I love to teach people who want to learn. The fall after graduating from college, I was asked to teach a course at a community college on the far South side of Chicago. Preparing to teach the class was daunting. Because it was considered to be a boring lecture class by students, I worked hard to make it a class they would benefit taking.

My efforts paid off, and each successive semester I was asked to teach another graphic arts class. Accepting the challenge each time eventually paid off in being hired to teach full-time in the Graphic Arts Technology Department. As an instructor on a tenure track, I was encouraged to go back to school and earn a Master's Degree.

Both my parents were teachers, so I asked my Mother what she thought about my going back to school to learn how to be a better instructor. She told me earning a degree in Education would not make me a good teacher. She assured me that I would gain insights, but either people are good teachers…or they are not. Undaunted, I enrolled in an Education MS program at Purdue University and specialized in Instructional Design.

Working full-time at the College, while I was going to school myself was not easy. I was tired, stressed, and yet I knew that my professional qualifications would benefit me in the long run. I was able to apply in my classrooms what I learned from my professors. Being able to determine what was likely needed for my students to learn and try it out was a glorious experience. The community college students were learning about graphic arts; I was learning about teaching. We all moved forward simultaneously.

The year was 1995, and it was an exciting technological time. The world was changing, much as it did with the invention of modern printing processes when Gutenberg invented moveable type. The internet was just starting to take off, and with a few clicks on a keyboard people could feed their curiosity with whatever they chose to learn. It became obvious that the internet had the ability to change us, change society and change the world as we know it.

Having freshly graduated with my Master's degree in Instructional Design, I was still teaching full time. I began to consider if it was possible to teach a class using the world wide web. It seemed like a fabulous idea to be able to teach students wherever they were able to access the internet… at home, at work… anywhere.

I searched to find if there were online classes I could take until I found one. I don't recall what the class was about, but I do remember it was a synchronous class that was taught using a chat room. The teacher would type in lectures and answers; we would type in questions.

One day I asked the teacher from what location he was teaching. He said he was near Seattle, sitting in his car, waiting in line for as ship to take him to Vancouver Island. He was using a satellite modem to access the internet and teach the class.

It blew my mind! And I knew in that instant I wanted to do what he was doing…teach from anywhere.

When the College Vice President put out a call for someone to lead the online instruction initiative at our school, I submitted my resume. Not only did I get the job, but I was also asked to come up with my new job title. Soon everyone knew that Pam Daniel was the college's new Online Instruction Specialist.

In my new position, it was necessary for me to teach other teachers how to teach their courses online. At the same time it was necessary to teach students how to learn in an online course. This multipronged issue, as it turns out, never ceased to be an ongoing challenge.

THE challenge for teachers was, and is, being able to adapt instruction methods to align with student learning styles, in a way that enables them to effectively learn. THE challenge for students was, and still is, adapting to instruction methods and managing their own effort. It's a tandem situation full of dilemmas.

As I began my journey as an explorer of the limitless potential that online learning offers, my new, but not young, supervisor said to me "Classes in technology teach people to do, not think."

My jaw dropped. I honestly remember it literally dropping with surprise. Then without a moments' more hesitation, I suggested to him that he keep that opinion to himself. The instructors in the technology department would be really insulted if he said that out loud. It was clear to both of us that he had just insulted me, and our stance shifted, our expressions became less congenial. Like my students, I am not a mindless monkey just learning how to press a button—the essence of technology courses require people to learn and think.

That naïve insult motivated me to expose how teachers from every discipline had to change their instructional methods, and how they think about teaching an online class.

My hope was there were other colleges I could learn more about online education and assessment. With optimism, I took the risk of leaving my tenured job at the community college in the Chicago suburbs. I was eager to find what more there was to learn. In doing so, I became the pushy new teacher, that expected to get the 'desirable' online classes to teach. Job after job, I struggled to use my skills and being involved in furthering the potential of online instruction.

At its core, online learning can be delivered synchronously or asynchronously. The teacher delivers content in a variety of ways: video, games, and works to develop a community of learners in each class. Communication between teacher and student is really important, and can take place via text, email, video chat or even social media. It is whatever the teacher chooses, and the students are most comfortable with using.

Each of us has our favorite way of communicating. Have you thought about how you learn best? My favorite ways to learn is by traveling with my husband, Dennis. I've visited forty-nine states, all except Oklahoma. I have flown to Germany, France, Belgium, and the Netherlands. The big take away lesson I've learned is people are more similar than we are different.

What we think we know about other states...other countries... is really what the governments are doing in those places and what we see and read in mass media. Knowing this reinforces my prime directive to see the world with my own eyes. Each of us is the eyes of our world, or at least we should be so.

Being trapped at home during Covid, we were desperate to go somewhere... anywhere other than the local grocery store. Dennis and I began to devise a way we could safely travel. We reasoned that if we traveled in an Amtrak sleeper car, we could avoid interacting with other people. We decided it was a viable option and agreed it was worth taking the risk. We made plans to travel west to San Francisco, California.

As the departure date drew near, an unexpected catastrophe occurred and forced us to reconsider our escape. Each day as we watched the nightly news on TV, we were shocked to see wildfires were spreading across the Sierra Nevada Mountain Range. Many of the fires were megafires—large, intense blazes that severely damaged landscapes and the communities within them. Later we learned the Dixie Fire was the largest single wildfire in California state history, burning nearly 1 million acres.

Despite the fires, we decided to go out west anyway. We felt confident that we could avoid any problems. And for the most part we were right. It was possible to generally avoid other people on our train journey by confining ourselves to our compartment.

We had lots of time to ride the train and look out the window. When I got bored of doing this, I used my phone as a hotspot to access the internet on my laptop. I was able to teach my online speech class from where I was. In that moment, I realized I had finally achieved my lifelong professional goal. That still sticks with me because it means that I can stop pushing so hard to further my skills at teaching online.

I can relinquish my sword and let others be the knights that push ignorance and barriers of online education over. Online learning is no longer unusual, it is at last just another mode that we can use to learn.

The revelation I had achieved my professional goal excited me and made me smile. I'd done what I had set out to do. I sat back in my seat to revel in the moment and looked out the window. What I saw was smoke in the trees, and I could barely see the mountains behind the trees. It took me a few moments to realize we were getting closer to the area affected by the wildfires. It was a clear and physical manifestation of the fact the world keeps changing.

One minute earlier and I felt as if I were on the top of

the world. Now I began to question where I'm going all over again. How brief is the sense of accomplishment. How vast are the possibilities in the world that we live.

I officially retired in 2019, yet I continue to teach public speaking online. The necessity of offering online classes during the pandemic has given me the opportunity to practice my craft and teach others a valuable skill. My students and I continue to connect meaningfully with each other using text, email and other tools. It does not matter where they are, or where I am sitting at my computer, we all continue to learn ways to be a better version of ourselves.

About the Author
Pam Kirchner Daniel

Pam is an actor, artist, activist, entrepreneur, actress and instructor of public speaking (LLCC). She loves to travel with her husband Dennis, and their happy place is Yellowstone National Park – specifically the first meadow of Slough Creek.

She is fierce and determined to teach others how they can share their truth.

Teach from anywhere.

Chapter 13

Vicarious Grief & COVID-19

By Sharron Magyar

About half-way through the COVID epidemic, I rolled out of bed feeling I had the burden of the world on my shoulders. A massive dense energy pushed in on me. It was heavy and oppressive. What curiosity—I felt fine yesterday.

Mourning bored down on me like black tar oozing over my skin, suffocating all the air out of my body. I continued through the day feeling the weight of the world, finally understanding I was feeling vicarious grief.

In 1987, a psychologist Robert Kastenbaum Ph D. coined the term vicarious bereavement. Vicarious bereavement is a continuing process of transition over time that results from witnessing or overhearing about other people's anguish and pain.

You bring their sorrow, fear, anger, and pain into your own recognition and experience when you identify with the agony of people who have suffered dreadful events. Your grief is real, even though you didn't know them.

Therese A. Rando (1997) defined "vicarious bereavement" as loss, heartache and mourning that arises following the deaths of others not known by the mourner. Vicarious grief refers to unhappiness prompted by someone else's loss. Most people's emotional make-up contains empathy.

Vicarious grief occurs in two types. The first type of pain is experienced as an observer. The mourner suffers extraordinary heartbreak for a person's loss and can have empathy for what they may have suffered.

In the second type of vicarious grief, the mourner is inside the grief, experiencing it both physically and emotionally. It is personal and up front. You may have headaches, heart palpitations, lethargy, and an inability to move beyond depressed thoughts.

I experienced the second type of vicarious bereavement; in that it was both physically and emotionally upsetting me. I was holding space for people experiencing the ravages of COVID-19.

There was loss after loss with COVID-19. People experienced grief, yet sorrow has many faces which are *complicated, disenfranchised,* as well as *vicarious* grief.

Foremost, there was the loss of loved ones because of COVID-19. Loss of your loved one is hard, but even more so during the pandemic for multiple reasons. Every day when we watch the news, there is an update on COVID cases reminding us of our continuing sorrow.

On the day of my overwhelming grief, my emotions magnified one hundred times. I bent under the weight of heartache. I had tapped into collective sorrow.

This grief was heavier, denser, unlike the sharpness of anguish I felt at losing my children. When I remained still and tuned into it, the differences were noticeable. Communal grief arising from the destabilized social economic systems and individual loss because of illness and death pushed in on my grieving heart.

Misery during COVID-19 exasperated our socio-economic systems as we could not deal with the burden of collective loss. In the United States alone, there were 214,000 children who lost their parents because of COVID-19. (San Francisco Chronicle, May 6, 2022) Most children who lost one, or both parents were under the age of 13.

American Indian, and Native Alaskan, Hawaiian, Pacific Islander children were hard hit. They lost their parents 3.5 times the rate of White children. Our heart was breaking for the children as we observed them suffering. Vicarious grief knows no boundaries.

One primary truth about life is we are in a flux of change. What is true of today will not be true of tomorrow. When you lose a loved one, the transitoriness of life etches on your heart, and it changes your outlook and relationships.

The breakdown of social systems made it hard to navigate burial, psychological and social support for those left grieving. Children are still reeling under the grief of their losses and trying to adapt to life without their parents. They were also struggling to live in a world without touch.

Loss of our ability to hug and touch our children, friends and family took a toll on each of us. COVID-19 was a great social leveler. It did not matter if you were rich or poor. What we learned through the COVID experience was we need people.

There are studies showing that touch soothes the heart and signals security and care. Basic loving touch quiets cardiovascular stress, releases serotonin and oxytocin, as well as elevates our mood. It also activates the body's Vagus nerve, producing our empathetic response.

We need touch and we grieve its loss when we don't get it. Sometimes you must reach out to those you feel comfortable with and ask for a hug or touch.

One of the biggest challenges with the COVID-19 experience was change was as rapid as a train barreling down the railroad tracks.

There was no stopping it. You could not jump off; It forced you to take the ride until it came to a screeching stop.

Your heart is in your throat with terror as you realize you are no longer safe. All safety in the world has disappeared and you have no control over what is happening to you. You are at more risk for grief when change is rapid and unexplainable.

Grief did not stop at the loss of our loved ones. We experienced a deteriorating economy, a failure in leadership, natural catastrophes, energy outages, and fires. During COVID-19, we were witness to the death of our cultural figures and replayed abuses, such as George Floyd and Brianna Taylor.

Any flaws to our cultural system, such as vulnerability to toxic workplace conditions and political dissidence, added considerable pressure on our grieving heart. Issues piling up on each other became complicated grief.

COMPLICATED GRIEF

The American public experienced loss after loss heaped up on death, resulting in complicated grief. Loss of loved ones, way of life and freedoms, hope, the ability to travel and loss of physical contact generated personal heartache. Sorrow, numbness, guilt, and anger all are part of the grieving experience. As one accepts loss and moves forward, emotions become calmer.

The difficulty with COVID grief was there were so many facets of it. Experiences accumulated, magnifying our heartache. Many were debilitating and did not improve, even after time passed. Emotions were so prolonged and severe that countless had trouble recovering from their losses and resuming their lives.

Shutdown of mental health systems added fuel to the fire. The psychological situation of the grieving heart yielded anxiety, stress, and sadness.

There were collective losses during COVID-19. Many had to deal with disenfranchised grief, which is bereavement not acknowledged or publicly and socially accepted. We deny mourning with disenfranchised grief. Researcher Ken Doka identifies disenfranchised grief as:

- Society does not recognize the loss as worthy of grieving.
- Person shows lack of response or over-exaggerated response.
- Death is because of suicide or overdose.
- Stigmatization of the relationship. (i.e.: Extramarital affair.)

Disenfranchised anguish often denies the ritual of the funeral process, which helps us to confront the reality of our loss and bring it to closure. As we each observed the statistics climbing on TV, our feelings of loss depersonalized.

Our hearts and brains checked out, and it overloaded us with pain. There was no way to process all the sorrow we were feeling. Denial of the opportunity to bring closure to our losses puts us at greater risk for complicated grief.

You might wonder what kinds of people experience vicarious bereavement? How did COVID-19 exasperate our experience of it? Everyone, if she or he feels empathy, can experience vicarious grief. The more a person experiences natural empathy, the more prone you are to vicarious grieving. Empaths sensitive to energy respond quicker to collective energy.

Identification with the victim in terms of age, circumstances, family situation, gender, and ethnicity can provoke vicarious grief. The more you have a situation similar, the greater the probability that vicarious grief will develop. This identification can also trigger personal unresolved bereavement.

When we witness others facing a loss like our own, it will set off personal sorrow over our own situation. We may compare the resemblance to the circumstances of death, the age of the victim, relationship to the victim, or the unpredictability of the death.

When my daughter lost her son, it brought up memories of losing my daughter and magnified my feeling of personal bereavement for her loss. In short, the presence and similarity of unresolved losses within us heightens our identification with the actual mourner, and thus increases the likelihood of vicarious grieving. The sheer volume of grief producing experiences of COVID-19 can lead to complicated grief.

People in helping professions—doctors, counselors and therapists, teachers, rescue workers, law enforcement officers, and lawyers—may be more vulnerable to vicarious grief.

Love is the glue that holds us together, yet love opens us to the possibility of being hurt. Any person who has a significant relationship with a survivor of trauma may feel secondary grief.

COVID-19 granted opportunities to confront our helping professions by presenting excessive workloads. High-stress circumstances, comprising of being on the front line, gave people the sense of defenselessness and no control. There were challenges with managers and employees. Many contended with a lack of justice or value or compassionate resolution of conflicts. Can you imagine how tough it was to choose between who lives and who dies because of lack of resources?

Quarantine from family or friends concerning the traumatic and challenging nature of one's responsibility enhanced pressure to an already stressful condition. All of us witnessing our traumas experienced vicarious grief. People in helping professions can reduce the risk of sadness and pain by practicing self-care.

What kinds of things can you do that will help you unplug? How can you take time to rest your mind? Retire into a quiet, still place and come into touch with your inner calm.

For myself, it is walking, reading, writing, and working on my art. Music, journaling, hobbies, and spending down time either by yourself or with family may help others cope with the mourning experience.

Women are at a higher risk for vicarious grief. It used to be accepted women were naturally more empathetic than men, but I question this belief in today's environment. Women have the advantage of being in tune with their children and babies, so perhaps they have more of an antenna for empathy.

Dr. Rando tells us grieving increases when children are involved. Most parents can imagine the anguish a parent must feel, and this often triggers fears for their own children.

People who fanatically watch the news media are at a higher risk for vicarious grief. The news media affects how and when we grieve. That is good and sometimes it is bad. Televised media, radio, newspapers, and information on our phones all serve as a catalyst for vicarious grieving. The media helps us grieve by urging observers to take part vicariously on occasions of shared loss or tragedy.

As humans, we are hard-wired to sympathize and communicate with others experiencing grief. It is common, although the experience varies in complexity from person to person. In this sense, the media delivers us with what we need and demand. What we have learned from the COVID experience is that we exhibit natural empathetic emotions and need to be connected to others in the world.

Science proves social isolation and loneliness links to greater risks for a variety of physical and mental conditions. High blood pressure, heart disease, obesity, a weakened immune system, anxiety, depression, cognitive decline, Alzheimer's disease, and even death are all by-products of loneliness. An especially destructive consequence of feeling isolated is mental decline and dementia.

We have compassion for other's stories, which touch our hearts and often break them. Loneliness exists in the world without others.

I believe there will be long-term repercussions of media overload with increased stories of trauma. The cumulative effect of vicarious grief puts us into compassion fatigue, injuring our mind, body, and spirit.

Every day the trauma we see on TV increases until we realize they have exposed us to too much violence, death, and loss in the American Culture. The long-lasting effect of over exposure is de-sensitization. How can we process our heartache if pain overloads us?

Think about this. Heartbreak has turned your safety in your world up-side-down. Anxiety becomes your bedfellow when you grieve. It is attempting to make you feel safe. The problem is you cannot trust anxiety during the grief process. When you lose someone, you can generalize loss and fear worrying about your others. Is there any logic to it? No, but your emotions are trying to make you feel safe.

Turn off the TV when you recognize you are absorbing too much trauma and violence. One problem with TV is violence and trauma present as images. Images carry a thousand words and sink into your subconscious mind to have a more negative impact.

Each person is different. Someone who has just suffered a loss of their loved one cannot tolerate observing others' anguish. They do not have the internal resources to process the emotions. Negative thoughts develop when your pain exceeds your capacity for dealing with suffering.

The way you move through vicarious sorrow depends on your unresolved individual pain and the quickness of the event activating the grief, your personal capacity to emphasize, and your social support system.

Give yourself time to be alone to process your feelings. Feel your emotions and work through them. Grief only becomes debilitating when your ability to call on personal resources diminishes. There may be wisdom to find someone who specializes in grief recovery.

PROCESSING AND SELF REFLECTION

COVID-19 helped us to develop resilience. I gave space for my day of mind-boggling vicarious grief. I allowed my body to feel it and gave permission for sorrow to cycle through me with hopes it could relieve someone else of heartache. There were many lessons in my experience. Foremost, being we are all interconnected and what one does affects the remaining. When you have empathy for someone who is grieving, they receive a kiss. One heart does impact another heart.

A second lesson is all emotion passes. Sometimes there is wisdom in observing them rather than reacting to them. When you are in the dark hole of sorrow, don't go chasing the rabbit into a dark ravine. Feel it, experience it, limit how far you will go with it.

A third lesson is to recognize when I am reaching a saturation point in observing other's trauma. Limit my exposure to news media when I feel that way. The world will still go around if I do not know the latest news.

Yet another lesson is to stay mindful and in the moment. What happened in the past is the past. What is going to happen in the future is the future. My hands are full living today. I must know when to say no and when to say yes. Learning when to say no and sticking to it is important. Maintaining firm boundaries is something I am learning to do.

Saying yes to the things that fill me up and guard my health is important. I don't have to be productive all the time. Perhaps I give myself permission to sit on the porch and admire the lake outside my door, doodle on my art, watch the children doing cartwheels. Oh, I can wear sweatpants all day if I want to.

Calling out the delights in every day is important. They are often little but more meaningful. When I stay in the moment, I appreciate the miracle of life and the flow and ebb of life and death. I want to live life to the fullest and I will embrace death as a part of life. Now I know I must ask myself, "What do I need?"

Grief can make you feel crazy, especially vicarious grief, because you rarely recognize where it came from. What could make me feel more supported and less alone? On the day I experienced the overbearing weight of vicarious grief, I needed to be alone and let it cycle through me. The next day I rolled out of bed, recognizing the grief had dissolved.

Have a resilience circle. Having those folks who'll be a sounding board and a cheer squad in your corner can get you through a lot. It doesn't matter how you connect — social media, zoom, letters all work the same.

Grief communities online, a grief circle or counselor can make you feel more comfortable admitting things you are reluctant to admit to yourself. Be honest about what is coming up for yourself and give yourself grace. There is no room for judgement with grief.

Sometimes it is not so easy to recognize vicarious grief from our personal heartache. It has specific characteristics often suddenly coming on and is out of context with what you are doing or experiencing. It can be a "curious" experience.

Your feelings are outside your normal thoughts, feelings, and processing. For example, if you vicariously grieve for your friend across the country, you may experience feelings of blueness, although everything is right with your world. You may get the notion to call your friend.

With vicarious grief, you could feel different emotions outside your normal experience of mourning. An example for me was I experienced anger with COVID-19 because I believed it was a man-made virus. I was also angry at the social and economic disparities I witnessed in the ability to access support. COVID-19 brought many disparities to light. Race, physical locality, political atmosphere of where you lived all affected the ability to receive medical and grief support.

When I experienced anguish in the situation in Ukraine, I also felt anger. Putin's decimation of Ukraine and complete disregard for life kept me angry. I felt little anger at the death of my children.

Emotions process to help us expand and grow. Following are ways to process your emotions:

- *Notice what feelings are bubbling up.* Is it anger, confusion, sadness? Examine if you feel more emotional or more detached.

- *Observe your emotions with objectivity.* Sit with your feelings without judgement and just let them cycle through you.
- *Tune into your body.* Where in your body do you feel your emotions? Do you have heaviness in your chest? Is a stomachache or a headache part of your physical reaction? Do you have shaky hands? Observe the emotions and let them be. The average emotion lasts sixty seconds. If we observe them and let them cycle through with compassion, we can witness the emotion as we release judgement or blame.

At the end of the COVID-19 experience, there was one thing that carried us through, and it is resilience. We knocked on resilience's door and walked through as a country and as a world. Vicarious grief affects our personal sense of self identity as a national identity. We have stepped into a new world and, like a snake, shed our skin to come out vibrant and colorful.

Our jobs, relationships, community, self-identity, and ability to give and receive love all affect our sense of self. We must redefine ourselves and move with the energy of change. The day of vicarious grief left me thinking about what we have learned from this experience and recognize there were specific characteristics that carried us through the door.

The first of those characteristics was our ability to adapt to change. We called in all resources both to combat COVID-19 from creating a new vaccine to have heated discussions of whether to mask or unmask. Even though we had conflicts, we maintained democracy and decency of human beings. Our morality mattered and our powerful sense of right and wrong came to the forefront of our lives.

There were many conflicts, but what stands out in my mind is the extraordinary compassion people showed to each other from rallying to provide food to others to supporting others in their moments of heartache in their loss of their loved ones.

Many reached out and dedicated their time and energy to a worthy cause, which helps to develop resilience. These moments were fine examples to our children. Others accepted what they could not control and looked for opportunities in the circumstances they were experiencing. There was unselfish concern for others.

Many of us cultivated resilience by adapting to the new work environment of working from home, connecting with others through zoom or other digital means.

We learned family matters much more than we realized. We also learned loneliness has its risks because it suppresses the immune system and can be the precursor to some diseases. People are a necessary part of our lives.

Optimism is a key component to resilience, and we clung to it like a baby clings to its mother. As a country, they gave us a monumental task of developing a vaccine under duress and figure out how to get it to the masses. Confidence and hopefulness prevailed, and it happened.

Many of us learned to quiet our minds and bodies. We learned to sit and enjoy nature. Time slowed, and we entered a vacuum of sound, sight, and inward thought. This is what it is to live in the moment. Each action counted, each reaction counted, and we were thoughtful. We questioned our spiritual beliefs and reconsidered what matters most in life. Those who could believe there is something bigger than themselves showed resilience.

Last, I have learned to practice gratitude to neutralize grief. Gratitude has a vibrational energy of 750HZ. Grief has a vibrational energy of 30HZ. You cannot feel both grief and gratitude at the same time. Gratitude grounds you in the present rather than focusing on what happened or worrying about what will happen in the future. Following are some tips for practicing gratitude:

- Start with the small stuff. As a hypnotist, I know change is more effective if you start small and at the beginning. Start your day before you get out of bed with thinking of three things you are grateful for. Little things are the foundation for gratefulness for bigger things.

- Be consistent and look to build more structure into your gratitude. Perhaps you journal each day or build a gratitude vision board. You can download a gratitude app on your phone to talk into each day. It is nice to see where you began and where you are.

- Note how far you have progressed. Check in weekly or monthly to note the patterns that are emerging. I know from the experience of writing a book at some point, the book takes on a life of its own. Your gratitude journey will take on a life of its own as well. As you progress, you will notice your grief lessening.

Many of the stories in this book tell everyone's personal walk with COVID-19. Like the experience with grief, it is personal and different for everyone. I will never forget my day of vicarious grief. It softened me; it expanded my perspective, and it helped me realize I am stronger than I thought I was. I understand I am in a place where I must look COVID-19 in the face with gratitude. I am changed and I think it is for the better.

Abhyankar, Lalita, M.D., M.H.S,
https://www.aafp.org/news/blogs/freshperspectives/entry/202001001fp-grief.html

Sullender, R Scott, Vicarious Grieving and the Media, Pastoral Psychology, volume 59, pages 191-200 (2010)

Hawkley, Louise C., Ph.D. and Cacioppo, John T., Ph.D., Loneliness Matters: A Theoretical and Empirical Review of Consequences and Mechanisms, Ann Behav Med, Author manuscript; available in PMC 2013 Dec 30.

About the Author
Sharron Magyar

Sharron Magyar is a visionary artist and consulting hypnotherapist who helps people to identify soul wounds that have them stuck in life. Her art and writing reach to the core of the self, as well as provide a path to wholeness. Currently she resides in Chatham, Il and is the owner of Golden Heart Hypnosis and director of Golden Heart School of Hypnosis.

Sharron's published book: *My Golden Heart: Putting the Pieces Back Together Again*

goldenhearthypnosis.com

sharronmagyar.com

I was in mourning.

Chapter 14

Life on the Edge: In Liminal Space

By Gloria Ferguson

Prolonged time in a doorway—between what was and what is to come—can be most unsettling.

In early March 2020, a friend shared fears about COVID-19, advising me to prepare for a worst-case-scenario pandemic. She recommended the purchase of a two-month supply of toilet paper, hand sanitizer, sanitary wipes, facial masks, disposable gloves, canned and frozen goods, and immune-boosting herbal teas and tinctures. Panic brewing, I decided to meditate.

A week later schools and nonessential businesses were mandated to close, and the Governor issued a stay-at-home order. Similar actions were taking place in other states across the country. My New Hampshire daughter called with stressful news...her husband's tent-and-event business was in financial crisis...and she had awoken in the night with a panic attack.

"I'm learning more about myself," she said.

Daily life was quickly changing. My weekly trip to the grocery store took far more emotional energy than usual, as I prepared myself with face mask and disposable gloves. Inside was an eerie scene of empty shelves and masked shoppers following red-taped arrows and other signs to maintain social distancing.

I felt like I had just stepped into an episode of *The Twilight Zone*. As I sheltered-in-place, I watched the daily news updates on coronavirus-related death tolls and surreal scenes of NYC's empty streets. To de-stress afterwards, I used combinations of Reiki, meditation and walks to the nearby park. Like my NH daughter, the abrupt life changes brought on by the COVID pandemic were revealing more about myself.

A people person, I soon began experiencing bouts of loneliness. I missed the company of my granddaughter, who I had been watching five days a week prior to the lockdown. Sheltering-in-place, sipping green tea while watching CBS This Morning news, I'd have flashbacks of other mornings—mornings that began with my granddaughter hiding under an owl-printed throw, waiting for me to poke the mound and say, "What is this? It looks like a mound of owls."

"Whooo, whooo, eeek, eeek," she replied.

Slowly revealing a hand, then a foot, she'd throw her cover off, and I would exclaim with feigned surprise, "It's Claire! My darling granddaughter Claire."

Then we would hug.

On the phone, my grandson pouted: "MeMa, I'm sooo bored. My friends are playing outside and—almost crying—I can't go over and play with them."

I empathized. With the cancellation or postponement of public Reiki events, private Reiki sessions and teaching Reiki classes—along with the loss of physical contact with family and friends—I felt very touch-deprived and cried more easily than usual. It was much harder than I imagined it would be.

An email from William Rand, founder and president of the International Center for Reiki Training (ICRT) introduced a way for teaching Reiki classes during the pandemic. The solution created for this included a distant Ignition (attunement) that would allow Usui/Holy Fire® III Reiki masters or Holy Fire® III Karuna Reiki® masters to teach classes online. I noted the date for William's online training for this, but I really did not feel drawn to teach Reiki online.

With the school closings and the stay-at-home order, the one year-from-retirement school teacher Stan and his 11-year-old son Quan practiced dribbling and shooting baskets together most every day. They lived two houses to the north of me and had a freestanding basketball hoop along our adjacent neighbor Vicky's concrete driveway.

Sometimes wife and mother Van would join them. I could see them playing from my kitchen window. Often the basketball would go over the fence and into my backyard. If I were outside, I would retrieve it. Most of the time Quan would climb over the fence.

Early in the pandemic, I went out to the fence to say hello and admire Van's cloth face mask—she always wore a mask around her family because she worked at a high-risk-for-Covid job. She was from Vietnam and struggled with her English. After sharing that I liked her face mask, she said, "I get you one."

Two days later, she sent her son over to deliver a cotton black-and-white patterned mask for me. Then, a couple weeks later, she sent her son over to give me another mask that she had made for me. It was a light blue cotton one, lined with white. Quan explained that his mom now had a sewing machine—so this was a better-made mask. She had hand-stitched the first one for me. The thought of her doing that made me teary-eyed.

It was during one of my de-stress walks in Lincoln Park in late March that I first spotted the pair of Canadian geese. They had returned to last year's nesting place— sheltering in a bed of tall iris blades near the pond's edge. Busily gathering twigs and leaves, they ignored me.

With the weather turning cold and windy again, over a week passed before my next trek to the park. A noisy disturbance at the pond signaled the arrival of eggs. On guard, in the middle of the road, the male goose was patrolling the area. A stopped car honked. The goose honked back, flapping his large wings.

Everything and everyone had now become potential danger to his mate and his future offspring. He chased after dogs, people, even other geese, enforcing strict social distancing. Amidst this outer commotion, the female sat quietly incubating her eggs, sheltering-in-place for the next 30 days.

In the park, I met a friend who was walking her dog and we chatted and strolled together. When we got sight of the pond, our conversation turned to the geese nesting at the pond's edge. I shared that this was their second year at the pond. She corrected me, saying that it was their third year at the pond. I was surprised. Must have been lost in my To Do List that summer.

The male goose saw us and crossed the road toward us, honking. My friend quickly moved farther away with her dog, while I bravely—or naively—continued at my usual pace along the walkway as the goose followed me. I could feel his beak touch my skin. I breathed a sigh of relief when I passed the pond's edge and he quit following me.

After this close encounter, I avoided the stretch of road near the pond. A global pandemic was enough stress, without being followed and threatened by a honking, nipping goose.

After a couple of weeks or so had passed, my curiosity got the better of me and I again walked the route near the pond. Three young adults, two women and a man were on the sidewalk beside the pond—very close to the nest. The male goose went into action, honking at them.

The women stepped back, but the man didn't. Instead, he began teasing the goose. One woman said, "Leave him alone. Quit messing with him."

The man reacted with a karate kick toward the goose, saying, "He doesn't scare me." After the kick, he rejoined his friends.

In mid-April, an online meditation from Richard Rohr, OSF—one of my favorite contemporary spiritual teachers—gave a new perspective on my/our turmoil, offering another way of viewing this crisis, which he referred to as "a global, collective liminal space".

Rohr described liminal space as either an inner state or outer situation that offers space for us to begin to think and act in new ways. We enter this "threshold place" of liminal space when we have left one room or stage of life but not yet entered the next.

It is often a time, he said, when our former way of being is changed or challenged, i.e., when we lose a job or a loved one, a major relocation, a serious illness, or the birth of a child. Rohr called liminal space a graced time that usually does not feel *graced* in any way, because, while in this space, we are not certain or in control.

In this threshold place, we are "free of illusions and false payoffs," he said, inviting us to "Discover and live from broader perspectives and with much deeper seeing."

As his words sank in, an inner peace came over me. I walked the park with deeper awareness of myself and my surroundings. As I took in the sky, the trees, the birds, and other walkers, I connected to nature in a way that felt surreal. The couple of Canadian geese nesting near the pond's edge again drew my attention—and a growing connection as I observed their lives unfold in the weeks ahead.

In spite of the rising death tolls, unemployment numbers and public discontent, I began focusing on "good" news—images of creativity, hope and promises of lessons learned. Tears of joy filled my eyes when pictures of unpolluted skies were aired from around the world, with reports that carbon emissions had dropped 17% globally. DW News from Berlin also reported that 68 German companies, including steel and chemical, had requested government direction on how to invest in climate protection.

And, on the BBC news, economist and banker, Mark Carney, reminded viewers that we can't self-isolate from climate change, as he spoke of the urgency of a green recovery.

THE CHAOS OF COVID

"The best way to find yourself is to lose yourself in the service of others," shared a smiling NYC nurse during an interview with a PBS reporter.

And, in China, a Wuhan student, after recovering from COVID-19, was happily donating his blood plasma (antibodies) to help someone else's recovery. Sharing with a PBS reporter what he had learned from his experience, he said: "People are precious, cherish everything you have, and be kind to everyone you meet."

After days of rainfall, I welcomed the sun and eagerly walked to the park. As the pond came in view, I noticed several people there, including a young man and his small son. The male goose was not barking or honking. It was quiet at the nest—something was different.

Coming close, I overheard the man tell his son that the chicks were all happy and content, taking a nice nap after swimming and eating. The goslings had arrived.

Speaking to me from across the road, the man said geese can be dangerous and related a sad story of a child who had had his eye pecked out by a goose. We talked a little more. I shared that this was the third year that this pair of geese had nested here, and that geese mate for life.

Sounding surprised, he exclaimed: "Really! So they've found a home here. I have more respect for them now."

At home, I turned on the news. More cases of COVID-19, more deaths. The Governor had extended the stay-at-home order to the end of May.

CBS Good Morning news brought more deaths and that unemployment had reached a record high. People were scared, angry, protesting stay-at-home orders. I decided to google Canadian geese.

Yes, they do mate for life; are extremely loyal and devoted mates, staying with an injured or dying mate even when the rest of their flock has moved on; and they have been observed grieving in seclusion when their mate dies—some spending the rest of their lives as widows or widowers, never mating again.

On my next walk in the park, as I rounded the curve, bringing the pond into full view, I came upon a young boy seated on the grass near the road. As I approached, he called out to another young boy who was walking down toward the west side of the pond: "What's the matter? What's wrong?"

The other boy didn't answer him. Instead, as he neared the pond, he picked up a rock and threw it. He then picked up another and threw it, and then another. I soon saw that he was throwing the rocks at the goose family who were standing in the tall grass near the pond's edge. He picked up a large stick and threw it at them.

As he picked up another, I yelled out to him, "Hey! Stop it. Those geese are protected by law."

I didn't look back but walked on past the pond and a couple seated on a bench near the east edge, who might have been the boys' parents.

Unsettled, I sought peace. I prayed for the troubled young boy, sending him and his family Reiki. I felt better. Camera bag hanging from my shoulder, I trekked over to the park pond the next day. To my relief, the geese were all safe, swimming together on the water.

I took pictures. A woman with kids were waiting for them to come to their side of the pond. They had pieces of bread to offer. No more threatening honks from the male—settled and friendly, he and his family eagerly took the bread offerings. It was a new normal. His seven little goslings were safe—at least, for today.

As the days passed, I would listen for the sound of the basketball hitting against the concrete driveway and look out my kitchen window to watch dad and son shoot baskets together. I didn't know at the time, but this too would change.

Memorial Day was approaching, and we still didn't know what the other side of this pandemic would look like. And yet, there was hope that we would get through this together and be better people for it. In the wise words of a famous poet (Poe), "Never to suffer would never to have been blessed."

Then, on Memorial Day, May 25, George Floyd, a 47-year-old black man, was intentionally killed in Minneapolis by a police officer. Caught on video, the public killing played over and over on all the news channels.

I sobbed each time I saw it, each time I heard Floyd's words, "I can't breathe." The sadness I felt was almost unbearable. Where's the grace of this, I thought.

In the wake of George Floyd's death, national awareness of the common prejudices and stereotyping of black males by those who were supposed to protect *all of us* from crimes of violence were being unveiled. In Minneapolis, black outrage was expressed in rioting, vandalizing, and setting fires.

Nationally, people of all colors took to the streets carrying Black Lives Matter signs, marching in protest to the injustices they had witnessed. George Floyd's death birthed a movement—a movement that spread quickly across the U.S. and to Europe and other countries in the world—countries who were seeing their own social injustices. It was a time of revealing. A time of uncovering that which was hidden—personally, nationally and globally. Lines from a Bob Dylan song played over and over in my mind, "the times they are a-changin."

Black Lives Matter signs began to appear in front yards around Springfield. The black couple across the street from me were the first in our neighborhood to display a sign and, to my surprise, the man smiled and waved to me.

In all the years that we had been neighbors, this was the first time that he had acknowledged me in such a friendly way. It felt good. I smiled and waved back.

About three months into the pandemic, I took a "leap of faith" and decided to teach Reiki in-person again and scheduled classes at my home for June and July, limiting the size to four students.

With social distancing during most of the training and wearing masks and frequent hand washings, we all safely got through the classes. Letting go of my fear and trusting that the students and I would be safe was a big step for me that summer.

In the fall, my neighbors Stan, Van and Quan contracted Covid. Mom and son got better quickly, but dad did not. Stan had to go to the hospital. He was placed on a respirator. As the days passed, I would ask my neighbor Vicky if she had heard how he was doing. The news was always the same—not better.

It was a quiet autumn. I missed their laughter and brief conversations at the fence. I even missed the pounding sound of their basketball hitting the concrete. I also regretted those moments of irritation when that sound interrupted my meditations or when the basketball would sail over the fence and land in my garden on top of a plant.

I had even shared my annoyance of this with my NH daughter. "Mom, don't sweat the small stuff," she replied, recommending a book for me to read with that title by Richard Carlson.

I had taken her advice and read the book out of curiosity. However, I still was not at ease with the possible loss of a plant or two. How trivial it all seemed now.

On my walks to the park, I would sometimes see them—mom and son—walking together. I would wave. The son would offer a little wave back. She would nod and bend her head down toward the ground, not wanting to make eye contact, not wanting to encourage conversation, not ready to share her concerns about her husband, who was still not better.

Late fall, I heard from Vicky that Quan was being allowed to go to the hospital to say goodbye to his dad.

As the CBS This Morning news ended, I again heard the reassuring words: "From our homes to yours, we can get through this together."

More comforting to me, however, were the hopeful words of Richard Rohr, that we were in a collective liminal space, a graced place betwixt and between what was and what is to come, a place where we could begin to think and act in new ways, a space inviting us to *discover and live from broader perspectives and much deeper seeing.*

It's been quite a journey...and it's not over yet.

About the Author
Gloria Ferguson

Gloria Ferguson is an Usui Holy Fire® III and Holy Fire® III Karuna Reiki® Master/Teacher, who has studied, practiced and taught Reiki for over 25 years.

Gloria can be reached by phone: (217) 544-4134, by email: gloria@reikiworks.org or on her website at:

www.reikiworks.org

Chapter 15

Here to Stay...Temporarily

By Jean Ferratier

Standing at the kitchen counter, with the array of prescription bottles in front of me, I methodically dropped a pill into the first of three separate weekly pill organizers. Filling the second one, I thought being painstakingly accurate is the most crucial and tedious part of getting ready for a trip.

I heard the 10 o'clock news on TV playing in the background. The anchor led with reports regarding a contagious disease called COVID, that originated in China. The number of people dying was increasing and slowly spreading to other countries from people traveling abroad.

Gathering my medicines to be packed in my suitcase, I thought how each day the news of the situation worsened. Like a stone thrown into a river, I wondered, how long would it be before its ripples impacted me? My attention then returned to preparations for my trip to Chicago from Springfield, IL.

My mood lifted while I gathered the wrapped birthday presents for my daughter and granddaughter. I was anxious to be on my way. I was highly anticipating this visit and had some important personal ideas I wanted to broach.

I was going to see Dani, Craig, Annya, and Warner. My children were finally living in close proximity. For several years, when one child moved to Illinois, the other would be living somewhere else.

Since Annya was born, rarely did I let a month and a half go by without a visit, in spite of the four-hour drive. I usually left on a Thursday to avoid Chicago weekend traffic, but more importantly, to be there on Friday to usher in Shabbat.

Welcoming the Sabbath with the beautiful Jewish rituals is one of the highlights of the week for our family. A tangible peace infuses the house, and tenderness spreads through me as each adult hugs one another acknowledging a moment of gratefulness.

Witnessing Dani and Craig bestow the traditional blessing for a child fills me with wonder. I picture Annya once cradled in her mother's arms as a newborn. I silently offer thanks that I have been present to marvel at her growth throughout the years.

Sundays, I packed to leave, unless there was a Monday holiday, which meant the kids had the day off from work and I had more time to spend with them. It was not uncharacteristic that I sometimes delayed departure an extra day because of a questionable weather forecast, or I didn't feel well, or maybe unconsciously I didn't want to go home.

Listening to spy thriller CDs borrowed from the library helped keep the drive from being so monotonous. No matter the time of day, traffic on I-55 through Joliet backed up. In order to keep panic at bay, entry onto the tristate necessitated changing an action-packed story to a calming instrumental CD, continuous chewing of M & M's, popcorn, or whatever the chosen snack companion was for that particular trip.

During the previous drive home from Chicago, in January of 2020, I was already thinking about my next visit. The end of February was Annya's birthday, and the beginning mid-March was Dani's and my birthdays. We decided in order to avoid driving up from Springfield for one celebration, only to go home, and drive back ten days later, I would plan a stay from February 20th through March 21st.

As I drove, I saw the miles in the rearview mirror taking me further away from my family. Heading towards Springfield, I reflected, whether after forty years, was I still content living there? It was an awareness to explore and seriously consider.

In the days before the February trip, I was observing that my feet were no longer firmly planted in Springfield. There were no relatives living in the area and even my ex-husband passed away years before. I had retired from the school district several years ago so there was no job holding me in place.

My very active social life had dwindled over the years. Although I had friends to meet with during the occasional dinner or movie, the groups that had nurtured my spirit and entertained me had diminished. Gone were the weekly Reiki and drumming sessions due to so many members moving away. I missed them, and I had not filled the gap of the spontaneous get togethers that we once created.

Ballroom dancing lessons were one of the last sparks of delight that I looked forward to during the week. For an hour or two, the cares of the world would slip away as I let the music and my dance partners waltz me around the floor.

Many of the students went dancing on the weekends, but those occasions happened less frequently as couples retired to other locations. Even I was less available because I had met a friend who enjoyed traveling and I was fortunate to go on cruises and vacations for weeks at a time.

Unforeseen opportunities were spontaneously appearing and like a butterfly emerging from a chrysalis, I was pleased to fly where the air currents might propel me.

I suddenly viewed my life in Springfield as a character in a fairy tale that started, *Once Upon a Time…*

I arrived in Springfield as a bride of three days. My husband, Lou and I tentatively planted seeds in a new town. At first, they were a bit dormant as I didn't think we would live there for more than a year. Springfield seemed a bit provincial after commuting to Chicago for a job at the American Heart Association where I felt I was making a difference and was well paid.

I had told my husband, I would only move if he got a job in a town that had a decent grocery store and at least one mall. White Oaks had opened the month before we were married, and I begrudgingly said that met the qualification.

THE CHAOS OF COVID

His internship job turned into a permanent one, and I guess I could say the rest is history. We were going to stay, so I reconciled myself to make friends, join groups, and to let the floundering seeds sprout. Two children, and decades later, Springfield was home with deep and tenderly cared-for roots.

Yet, I was growing restless. Instead of looking forward to coming home, I was planning for the next time I would leave to see family, friends, attend a spiritual retreat, or vacation. Like rubbing sleep from my eyes, I fully awakened, or maybe better said, stopped denying that I was ready to close one chapter and open another one in a different location. I had plans for my future percolating in my mind.

The morning of February 20th, I surveyed the trunk, mentally ticking off the checklist of medications, CPAP, luggage, and gifts. The presents were wrapped as cheerfully as my mood. I slammed the trunk and kicked the snow from my boots. Anything I had forgotten could be purchased or ordered later.

I was eager to be on my way, and I watched the garage door close thinking that when the door opened again in a few weeks' time, I might start disposing superfluous knick-knacks and setting a mental time frame of putting the house on the market.

Part of my plans depended upon my children's reaction to my idea to buy a condominium in the vicinity of where they lived. I already was familiar with the area and had friends in the region. My intuition led me to believe that the groundwork was laid to create a successful and happy move.

I would not make the mistake of buying a new residence until my home was sold as I had once before. Paying two mortgages was disastrous to my income. I could reside between Warner and Dani's home until I found a place of my own.

Hour after hour during the car ride, my thoughts flipped back and forth between seeing everyone, anticipating Annya's excitement unwrapping her presents, various events scheduled, the progression of COVID, and of course, the *Big Moving Discussion*. Trusting that once the conceptual plan was unanimously affirmed, it would be enough to get the energetic ball rolling. I was counting on the Universe to guide and lead the way.

When I arrived, I hauled all the items from the car into Dani's house. It would be an hour before the family came home from work and daycare pick-up. Two-years, but soon-to-be, three-years-old, Annya had not been told I was coming. I couldn't wait to see the surprise on her face to see me when she walked in the door.

The next evening, we drove to Warner's home for Shabbat dinner. He had moved in only four months before, and it was still a novel event for us all to be there at once. I didn't take it for granted how wonderful it was to gaze at everyone around the table as the blessings were chanted, and songs were sung. Even Jack, Warner's dog, seemed to participate as his tail slapped against my leg from where he laid under the table.

We talked, ate Warner's special apricot chicken, and tried to keep Annya occupied at the table. I hoped this was just the beginning of many Fridays we would spend together. That night, much of the conversation centered around plans for Annya's upcoming birthday celebration.

THE CHAOS OF COVID

We were all looking forward to her party and the arrival of out-of-town guests. So far, everyone we knew was healthy and had not been exposed to COVID.

We didn't know much about the disease, but we all recognized how the topic was becoming more frequent in the news and our conversations. Hearing of the increasing numbers of known cases, hospitalizations, and death alarmed us. Although our lives went on routinely, there was a feeling like a dark fog was creeping up to our door. Worldwide, COVID was advancing, and there was no denying the treachery in its wake.

Annya's birthday arrived and fulfilled our desires for a memorable day. Young and old alike joked while painting popsicle stick picture frames. Annya's face covered in orange and white frosting made us laugh, and we were delighted in watching her open her presents. It was hard to tell who was more excited with her play kitchen, Annya or the aunts and uncles who gave her the gift.

The following days passed quickly. I especially enjoyed going to the Chicago Botanical Gardens with my friend, Cathy, who once lived in Springfield. My eyes feasted on the numerous displays of vibrant colored orchids. The intricacy of their beauty was breathtaking, and I snapped hundreds of pictures to later be viewed in my photo album.

After the Gardens, we treated ourselves to lunch at The Cheesecake Factory. Following the hostess to the table, we couldn't help viewing all the assortments of cheesecakes on display, one of my favorites being the white chocolate raspberry.

After ordering our meals, I told Cathy I was thinking of moving to be near my children, as she and her husband had done. She imparted a wealth of information regarding their adjustment, the new groups she joined, and social opportunities offered through places like libraries, book clubs, and performing art centers.

My birthday dawned with a day filled with treats. Aside from a family dinner party, Warner and Dani surprised me by taking me to dine at the Chocolate Sanctuary restaurant. Our mouths watered as we read the rich and decadent menu offerings.

Over a slice of Heavenly Dessert Cake delivered by the restaurant staff in honor of my special day, I broached the subject of my moving to the area. My children were neither astonished or shocked, and stated that they had already discussed it a few times. That left me slightly stunned.

I was under the impression that they liked when I came to visit but had not perceived they welcomed my moving near them. They explained that while they supported me locating in the area, they did not embrace the idea of me living with them. I laughed and stated that we were all profoundly in agreement on that point.

Conversation swiftly turned to brainstorming the possible where, when, and how of putting plans into place. First steps proposed were to contact the real estate agent with whom we had worked in the past when I returned to Springfield. Getting the house decluttered and ready to be shown could begin immediately with a projected listing date in May or June.

My birthday lunch was deliciously unique and satisfying. We parted ways knowing we would meet up again the following week to celebrate Dani's birthday.

Wanting to provide some humor and fun along with birthday cake, Dani invited family and friends to an afternoon of painting ceramics at a pottery shop. We were a noisy group, teasing and encouraging each other, while painting our projects. Once completed, we left our items at the shop to be glazed. We had no idea it would be several weeks before we could pick up our pieces because the shop would be closed indefinitely due to COVID restrictions.

My trip was drawing to an end. My mind and heart were full of filed-away memories from the last few weeks. This time, packing to go home, I felt content and purposeful. I had ideas and strategies in mind for decluttering the house. I already pictured rummaging through closets pulling out clothes to be donated.

Everyone was at work when I was ready to leave. I lugged the suitcase, the CPAP, and new packages into the trunk. I slipped into the driver's seat blissfully unaware that in a few moments Divine Intervention was about to start throwing curve balls into many anticipated and wished-for plans.

Backing out was awkward and challenging for whomever parked on the left of the three-car garage. No matter how many times I had done it before, it never got easier to navigate the sharp turn needed to avoid rolling onto the grass planted on an angle of the limited blacktop driveway.

I inched the car back slowly, slightly turning the wheels to avoid scraping the side view mirror when I heard a screeching, dragging sound. I couldn't imagine what happened.

Reluctantly, I turned off the ignition, and walked around the car to see that the right bumper had hooked onto a stroller that had been placed in the narrow area between the parking spaces. I dislodged the stroller, but in doing so, pulled the bumper leaving it hanging precariously off the car. I had also jarred the garage door track, bending it slightly.

My stomach plunged knowing I had to call Dani and Craig and tell them about what I had done. They reacted more calmly than I expected, even as my heart continued to race, not knowing how to remedy the situation.

Dani told me to wait in the car while she and Craig called each other to discuss what should be done. At that point the car was half in and half out of the garage.

After a few minutes, Dani called me back and said I should drive my car to a body repair shop down the street for estimates. Enterprise was right next door in case a car rental was necessary. I popped the trunk and dragged all my belongings back into the house before cautiously heading out.

A quick evaluation of the bumper revealed it might be possible to drive to Springfield, but if I hit any pot holes, it could fall off. They recommended a new bumper and if they could find a replacement, it might be ready in three days. Trudging next door to Enterprise, I rented a car to buzz around town. It didn't make sense to drive home, when hopefully the car would be repaired in a timely manner.

They did find a replacement bumper, but it would require a paint job delaying my departure another day.

THE CHAOS OF COVID

This was beyond my one-day extra bonus that usually accompanied previous visits. Mentally and physically, I was ready to go. I had appointments in Springfield that would need to be rescheduled.

I could wash my clothes, but I had only a few days of medications left. The reports of the contagious nature of COVID with no known treatments available were dominating the news cycles, and I wanted to make it back safely to my own home.

Late Thursday afternoon, the car was ready. I returned the rental and drove back to Dani's house. Another Friday was approaching and Dani, Craig, Annya, and I, were invited to welcome Shabbat with dinner again at Warner's. I would spend the night at his home since it was closer to the tollway and leave for Springfield early the next morning.

Friday arrived and I once more loaded the trunk. It was beginning to feel like a scene straight out of the Groundhog Day movie, reliving the same actions over and over.

The aroma of brisket wafted from Warner's kitchen while we waited for sunset so we could light the Shabbat candles. We sat in the living room chatting about this and that when our conversation turned to more serious topic of COVID.

Craig said he was informed by his company that there was a possibility that everyone might have to start working from home to prevent the spread and contamination of the disease. There were hints circulating that as preposterous as it sounded, Americans might be told to quarantine by sheltering in place. The implications of how that could affect every aspect of our lives were too numerous to conceive.

I reasoned it was a good thing I would be leaving the next day, but the children had concerns. Apparently, they had heard about the possible quarantine, and they were uneasy that I would get home and would be isolated for an unknown length of time. COVID was now referred to as a pandemic, and daily life would be challenging in ways we have never encountered.

I didn't argue the merits of their compelling suggestions to stay. Scenes raced across my mind of being alone day after day and managing on my own. I was grateful that my children cared so much about my well-being.

I had been upset about the car smashup but suddenly saw the event in a new light. Had that slight collision not occurred I would have been left to face an uncertain future on my own. I silently thanked G-d for the blessing of a broken bumper that caused my delay in leaving.

The atmosphere during dinner was subdued. Innately, I understood that we were sensing significant changes approaching, and circumstances that began as little waves might turn into a tsunami the likes of which we never imagined in our lifetime.

I was looking at Warner when the first crashing wave nearly knocked me off my chair. Once we departed that evening, when would we be able to see him again? In reality he lived minutes away from Dani and Craig, but during a lockdown, it would feel like he lived in another state.

Tears welled in my eyes as I hugged him good-bye. Something precious was being taken away from me, from every individual who wanted to be near a loved one.

It would be only a few weeks before COVID would run rampant in nursing homes and the elderly would endure the loneliness of being confined to their small room. Even more heart-wrenching, many stricken with the disease died alone in their hospital rooms due to strict no-visitor policies.

I followed Dani, Craig, and Annya back to their house. I popped open the trunk and once again unloaded my suitcase and CPAP. I crossed the threshold wondering how long this unplanned stay would last?

By Monday, Craig was told to work from the house. Annya's daycare was still open, but her parents felt she would be more protected at home by not being exposed to other children.

I spent the day talking to my mail order prescription provider explaining why I needed to order a supply of all my medications, placing mail forwarding with the post office, and calling neighbors and friends to let them know it would be a while before I would be back.

The government shelter-in-place recommendation came before we were ready. I bet I was not alone in wishing I had gone to the grocery store, had my haircut, seen a friend, or a myriad of other things one last time.

Now Dani was also working from home, and I was glad I could help watch Annya. Missing her daycare friends, I frequently heard Annya's refrain, "Ga-Ga, will you play with me?"

Each day, more restrictions were put in place as the virus spread globally. Schools, restaurants, malls, air travel, and places of worship were shut down. Medical supplies were in short supply, and it was frustrating that even simple face masks were unavailable due to global shortages. Stocks plunged daily.

There was no end in sight, and we hoped the infectious disease doctors appearing daily on TV could provide guidance for safety and treatment.

Instead of in-person communication, computer Zoom technology became commonplace. Even the technologically challenged became computer savvy in order to find connections to others.

It became apparent that the quarantine would extend well beyond the initial two weeks. It was winter, and it was strange to stay inside every day. Dani would stay up late trying to get on the Shipt list to place orders for food.

When delivered, groceries were dropped off at the front door, and we wiped down every item with disinfectant before it came into the house. Eventually, I conceded to order more socks and underwear from Amazon.

Hospitals were over-flowing with the sick, and temporary morgue space needed to be constructed. Non-life-threatening procedures were canceled. When I endured a painful back flare-up, I had to schedule time to speak with a health professional over the phone since in-person doctor visits were unavailable.

We had challenges, but not the hardships many Americans were encountering. Many were in crisis not having work, childcare, or availability of food. Schools that provided breakfast and lunch for low-income students were closed. On T.V., we saw miles of cars waiting in lines to pick up donated life-saving groceries.

THE CHAOS OF COVID

Winter passed to spring and we, like millions of others, were still sheltering in place. I was frustrated that I couldn't go home. With the arrival of warmer weather, I needed to order lighter weight clothing. I had come to visit, but even my temporary stay had no end in sight.

I still wanted to get the Springfield house on the market, and the only progress I had made was to have the real estate agent walk through the house. She let me know what would be required to prepare the house for showing and a possible sale price. I wanted to sell, even though I knew I would not look for a place of my own until the pandemic was over.

The economy was taking a hit and unemployment numbers kept rising as businesses continued to be closed. Many organizations reevaluated their budgets and implemented staff cuts. It was shocking when Dani's job was eliminated with only a few days of warning. First there was disbelief, then outrage, followed by concern. Like many other families, we wondered what changes we might have to implement in the face of her termination.

In June, Dani and I decided to make a three-day trip to Springfield, leaving Annya with Craig. We packed groceries and everything we anticipated needing so we would not have to enter public areas with the exception of refilling the car with gas.

Our intention was to collect clothes and items I wanted to take back to Dani's, and to declutter and pack as much as we could in the time available. Moving boxes that I had ordered ahead of time were waiting on the front porch.

We started working in the basement, sorting things into three piles: keep, sell/donate, and trash. We worked practically non-stop. I was amazed, and proud of myself, when I recognized how unattached I became to my things as I considered how much it would cost to have an item packed and moved.

We accomplished a great deal, but soon it was time to leave, and there was so much left to do. My neighbor and her sisters came to our rescue. Carefully masked and socially distanced, I invited them over to say good-bye and view our efforts.

I was beyond thrilled and relieved when they offered their services for hire to pack up the house. We agreed on a system where they would take pictures and we would facetime discussing what to box and what to pitch.

Dani and I drove back feeling tired but pleased with our progress. We were reassured that the packing would continue.

Within three weeks, enough boxes were packed, and trash removed to allow the house to go on the market. Remarkably, houses were selling fast, even during a pandemic. Realtors put precautions into place so people could safely view a home by keeping strict appointment times, masking, limiting surface contact, and leaving closet doors open. On websites, virtual tours were offered.

It is said that a home's location and correct price-point is key to selling quickly and that was true for me. A huge weight had been lifted when a contract was signed with a closing date set for two months. I was in limbo, but soon the house would not be a responsibility for me.

One night during dinner, Dani said she and Craig were thinking of moving back to South Carolina. I thought they must be joking as this newsflash was delivered out of nowhere. I was numb with disbelief, confusion, and uncertainty. What about my plans?

They reasoned that Dani presently was not working, and Craig could perform his job from any location. This was an opportune time to move, and they hoped I would join them.

They had loved living in the South. They only relocated to the Chicago area because Craig had been offered a job upon graduating from the University of South Carolina. Every winter they wished they were back in the warm climate of the South.

COVID was still a major threat with no cures available, and a return to normalcy wasn't within reach. Still house-bound in summer, we occasionally saw people by sitting at opposite ends of the front yard. Yet, we didn't enter other people's homes or go anywhere. I was still a temporary resident for the foreseeable future.

In February, when I thought of moving, South Carolina was not even a blip in our consciousness. Now, I had sold my home, and would not buy another in the foreseeable future. If and when Dani and Craig moved, I felt it was my best option to go with them.

I never dreamed of living in the South, and I despondently watched my plans burn to ashes. The pandemic was unraveling the safe and secure life I knew. I wondered if the Universe had something in store for me.

I didn't think Dani and Craig were contemplating a change quite so seriously and quickly. I had a hard time adjusting to the idea of moving out of state, and leaving Warner, just when he had moved closer.

Once their decision was made, they put their house on the market and traveled to South Carolina to buy a house. Dani started looking for jobs.

By the end of August, movers were packing up Dani and Craig's house. I coordinated with the movers in Springfield for the same time. I had made arrangements for some of the furniture to be sent to Warner and the rest to the new house in South Carolina, with the overflow going into a storage unit.

We have been living in South Carolina now for one and a half years. There have been many silver linings. Despite saying I would not live with my children; it has been a blessing. They loving welcomed me into the daily fabric of their lives, encouraging me to think of their home as my home.

Their attitudes, and the sight of seeing my furniture from Springfield incorporated with theirs indeed makes me feel *home*. Our bonds of connection have grown and strengthened. I laugh when they jokingly tell their friends that they have joint custody of Mom.

I like the warm weather, especially when I hear about snow in Chicago. I adore the old Southern homes with their welcoming porches. Slowly, I am learning my way around the area, but GPS is turned on for reassurance.

I am adjusting to the area, but social life is limited. Although I have had two vaccinations and two boosters, COVID variant cases are on the rise, causing me to consider my outings carefully. For the last few months, we are able to move around more freely, but we are still masked and socially distanced.

The pandemic has profoundly changed people's priorities with living locations being one of them. There is a housing shortage, and interest rates are on the rise after an all-time low. It is not feasible for me to buy a home yet. I am resentful that COVID still runs the show in directing facets of my life such as where I live and with whom I feel I may safely interact.

So, for now, if you want to visit me, I am in South Carolina living with Dani, Craig, and Annya. I am here to stay, temporarily.

About the Author
Jean Ferratier

Jean Ferratier, a retired teacher, is a Mindfulness Heart-Centered Life Coach and Archetypal Consultant. She enjoys writing personal memoirs and is a frequent contributor to Chicken Soup for the Soul Books.

She also has a deep interest in the metaphysical and has authored Reading Symbolic Signs: How to Connect the Dots of your Spiritual Life.

She enjoys teaching about and sharing orb photography. Hobbies include dancing, quilling, attending theater, and of course, playing with Annya.

Chapter 16

The Fear Pandemic: Collective Fear During the Time of COVID

By Justina Schacht

I am afraid I am going to get COVID and die.

I am afraid my spouse will get COVID and die.

I am afraid my child/children are going to get COVID and die.

I am afraid my parent/parents will get COVID and die.

I am afraid my grandparent/grandparents will get COVID and die.

I am afraid someone in my family will get COVID and die.

I am afraid I will get COVID and inadvertently give it to a family member, and they will die.

I am afraid it will be my fault.

I am afraid I will have to stay home forever.
I am afraid I will have to go back to the office.
I am afraid I will never have human touch again.
I am afraid I will never have sex again.
I am afraid I will run out of toilet paper.
I am afraid I will run out of food.
I am afraid the grocery stores will run out of toilet paper.
I am afraid the grocery stores will run out of food.
I am afraid the country will get shut down.
I am afraid some stranger will give me COVID, and I will die.
I am afraid I will give COVID to my pets.
I am afraid I am drinking too much.
I am afraid I am smoking too much pot.
I am afraid I am doing too many drugs.
I am afraid of not being able to cope anymore.

I am afraid I will never be able to go to a restaurant again.
I am afraid I will never be able to go shopping again.
I am afraid I will never be able to go out with my friends again.
I am afraid I will never go on a date again.
I am afraid people around me are unvaccinated.
I am afraid people around me have not gotten a booster.
I am afraid the vaccine will give me a disease.
I am afraid I won't be able to have children if I get the vaccine.
I am afraid I am going to die alone.
I am afraid my loved one will die alone.

THE CHAOS OF COVID

I am afraid our last words will be through an iPad.
I am afraid of being left alone.
I am afraid my life has no value others.
I am afraid my needs are not respected.
I am afraid to let my children go to school.
I am afraid my children will have to be home another month.
I am afraid one of my teachers will die of COVID.
I am afraid of being on Zoom.
I am afraid to teach online.
I am afraid if I turn on my Zoom camera, my teacher will see what kind of place I live in.
I am afraid my parents will embarrass me while I am in my Zoom class.
I am afraid if I turn on my Zoom camera, my professor will see that I live in my car.
I am afraid of being responsible for someone's death.
I am afraid to travel.
I am afraid to use public bathrooms.

I am afraid we won't be able to have a graduation ceremony now.
I am afraid to go outside.
I am afraid I won't be allowed to travel.
I am afraid I won't be able to travel again.
I am afraid the world will shut down.
I am afraid when we do go back to school that my friends won't like me anymore.
I am afraid I will give COVID to one of my coworkers, and they will die.
I am afraid I will not make it through another shift at the hospital.

I am afraid one of our customers will give me COVID, and I will die for this minimum-wage job.

I am afraid to see anyone else die at the hospital today.

I am afraid I won't be able to find a job.

I am afraid to work for myself.

I am afraid I will not be able to pay my rent.

I am afraid I will not have enough money.

I am afraid I will lose all my clients.

I am afraid I have become a Netflix addict.

I am afraid I will be lonely forever.

I am afraid I will never meet anyone.

I am afraid people will not wear their mask properly.

I am afraid people will tell me to wear a mask.

I am afraid...all the time.

I am afraid of going to the doctor.

I am afraid of being stuck in my dorm room all year.

I am afraid I will have to stay with my parents forever.

I am afraid to move to a new city. What if there is an outbreak there?

I am afraid of celebrating the holiday with my family.

I am afraid of staying here.

I am afraid life will never be normal again.

I am afraid of going to the gym.

I am afraid I will never have the level of energy that I did before.

I am afraid this brain fog will never go away.

I am afraid I will never be the same.

I am afraid to live when so many have died.

THE CHAOS OF COVID

I am afraid I will never be able to concentrate or focus again.

I am afraid I will lose my freedom if we all must go back to normal office life.

About the Author
Justina Schacht

Justina Schacht is a partner in Flow: Midwest Yoga & Meditation and the owner of Three Sisters Ayurveda. She began practicing yoga in 2006 and has been teaching yoga for over ten years.

Justina has a Bachelor of Arts degree in Literature and Communications and a Master of Arts degree in Liberal and Integrative Studies, Consciousness and Transformative Literature (South Asian literature and philosophy). Justina began leading Yoga Alliance-approved 200-hour teacher training in 2009, and Yoga Alliance approved 300-hour teacher training in 2018.

In addition to yoga postures, breathwork, relaxation techniques, and meditation, her teaching methods encourage holistic health and compassionate self-study through literature and writing.

Justina is an Ayurvedic Practitioner. The timeless wisdom of Ayurveda, the system of complementary medicine of India, is universal and applicable to everyone as it encourages natural well-being. Ayurveda uses a combination of nutrition and lifestyle changes, herbal medicinal preparations, healing oil treatments, yogic practices and purificatory treatments to alleviate a huge array of ailments, physical and mental. Restoring you to your natural balanced state means you can truly enjoy and fulfill your purpose in life.

www.threesistersayurveda.com

Chapter 17

Parents Paralyzed by the Pandemic:
Two Unique Survival Stories of
Two Pandemics

By J. Lieswald

What does an eleven-year-old boy in Oklahoma in the 1950s have in common with a thirty-nine-year-old woman in Illinois in 2020? They both survived pandemics, but in two completely different ways.

The thirty-nine-year-old woman would become the daughter of the eleven-year-old boy some thirty plus years after he became paralyzed from polio. How would that aid this woman to survive the COVID pandemic in 2020?

Being raised by a quadriplegic father who became paralyzed by his pandemic helped the woman become the person she was meant to be. She had the resolve to not only survive the COVID pandemic but prevent anyone in her household from falling ill, even when she got diagnosed herself in 2022.

In 1948 my father, Emmett H. Lieswald was nine years old when the first strand of polio hit his hometown of Alva, Oklahoma. He was one of the many children who became stricken with Polio, not once but multiple times.

My father shared his memories of his diagnosis at a young age with such a life altering medical condition. He recalled feeling like he was going to die young and never get a chance to grow up and get married. He was scared of constant testing with lots of needles along with radiation from multiple lab work ups and weekly scans.

He was treated for one problem and sent home for observations just to turn the car around, go back to do more testing to find a whole new problem he would end up enduring. Over the next two years he would find himself to be diagnosed with different strands of Polio, the next carrying a worse set of symptoms then the last.

What his family wouldn't give to have a healthy son who ran around pestering them with young boy problems just for one day. Little did they know, that would never happen again.

The painful memory of his parents putting him in the car that day to take him to the hospital has stayed present in his mind every year he survived another trip around the sun. Although I remember the conversation vividly, I do not recall the specific day.

I am certain he remembered. I mean who wouldn't after all he went through? While he was having muscle weakness and unable to stand up on its own, he slowly and unsteadily got out of the car and with some help turning from the nurse to sit down in the wheelchair brought to the car.

There, just inside the hospital lobby, the nurse helped him stand up from the wheelchair, again slowly turn around and cautiously sit on the gurney behind him. When he laid down and got comfortable, they raced him off to the lab for blood tests and an array of imaging tests.

His parents and the doctors were not prepared for what was to come shortly after the results compiled from the day's tests. While his parents were discussing the lab work and imaging results from his tests, my father's life completely changed course.

He had another attack while in the hospital that consisted of tingling and numbness in his hospital bed. As he went to try to shake his legs and arms to make them wake up and realized he could not lift any of his limbs he began to panic.

It felt like an anvil sat on his lungs when he tried to yell for help. His parents and doctors were just outside his room in the hallway and heard him gasping for air as his lungs were collapsing. He was able to get their attention by shaking the bed with his body and moaning.

The third Polio virus had attacked his spinal cord while a different strand of Polio attacked his lungs. He was unable to breathe or move on his own. He was rushed to the Emergency Room where he was placed into an iron lung until his lung and chest muscles were strong enough for him to be able to breathe on his own.

My father recalled the sensation of feeling like he was in a room with a bunch of science experiments as he was rolled from the emergency area. They took him to a big room where they kept all the patients that were in iron lungs fighting for their lives.

He suggested it looked a lot like a graveyard with coffins above ground. The iron lungs beeped, and with each pump of oxygen into each machine it would make a whoosh sound followed by a pop sound he described.

This was not something he had ever read in the newspapers or heard on the radio before. He was not sure what was going to happen to him. He had a thought that maybe they were new torture chambers, or maybe a fancy rocket to ship the sick off to the moon? The imagination of a young child could take them anywhere, especially when scared and isolated.

He thought about the other sick kids as robots with human heads looking at themselves in mirrors. There were more children than elders in those machines, and back then most of the patients did not make it out of them alive.

My father was one of the lucky ones of that early age to survive. He was permanently paralyzed from the neck down at age eleven by the time he was discharged from the hospital. He may have escaped the iron lung, but he was told he would be fortunate to survive long enough to see his twenties.

My father talked with his family before he was even a teenager about trying to preplan his funeral, but they did not have the money to do such a thing. There were too many medical bills over the past couple years.

The dream of an eleven-year-old boy and his family during summer break was not to find himself isolated inside an iron lung. This monstrous, enormous metal machine with windows, pumps, and a mirror to see himself and just a little bit of the kids around him.

His metal prison went on for months, and he went through physical and respiratory therapy for over two years. His parents wondered every day when he could go back to school. They prayed he would get through the awkward stages of puberty, with an acne-filled face, looking for a girlfriend like most other boys were so lucky to be experiencing.

Over three years of fighting the battle against Polio, his parents were looking at their new life of caring for a permanently disabled child. They were financially in despair and thought his future was in jeopardy. They had no idea how long they would get to care for him.

The doctors and his parents underestimated the power of his willingness to succeed and his ambition to prove them all wrong. Resilient, Emmett Lieswald lived for another sixty years. He graduated high school, completed college with multiple degrees, advanced in his career as an Administrator for several skilled nursing facilities, got married at twenty-two, adopted a daughter, and retired at sixty-eight. His biggest joy was becoming a grandfather.

In 2009 my father passed peacefully in his sleep the night he met his granddaughter for the first time. I like to think that is what he was living for all those years. He was seventy and my mother was turning fifty in just two days when he went to sleep forever.

He lived an amazing, full life of achievements just like any other kid would his age. He had high school girlfriends, earned college degrees, became the head of many skilled nursing facilities, married, had a child, divorced, retired from the State of Illinois, and died the night he met his first and only granddaughter.

Not to mention, he survived his life expectancy four time longer than predicted when he was eleven. You could say I get my strength, courage, and determination to succeed from being a 'Daddy's girl' and was always by his side. My father gave me all I needed and more when he was alive for me to be able to take on my families own worries that would arise just about a decade later after he passed.

COVID-19 is a deadly virus that was spreading remarkably fast, turning into a global pandemic, and within mere weeks shutting the entire world down for months. The world was changed forever.

He surely would not have survived this one, but thanks to his resilience, my family and I did survive. Changed, but harder and wiser for the experience. My father never hugged me, held me, picked me up, or even spanked me, but because of all his patience, determination, guidance, nurturing, and love I have so much support to give to those around me.

As a very young child I was always told by my mother, who was a nurse, the importance of washing my hands, keeping areas clean, and how to dress wounds properly to avoid getting my father sick. His immune system was compromised from being paralyzed for so long. He was six foot one, about two hundred pounds and with absolutely no extra lung or chest muscles to cough. Therefore, it was important to make sure my father stayed healthy.

Because of my father's compromised health, if someone were to become ill, we would make every attempt to distance my father from exposure. We were extra diligent about washing our hands before and after touching items moved from one room to another.

For example, when we would move a TV from the living room into my father's bedroom, we would wipe down the TV, wash our hands, move the TV into his room.

There were many times he would get so sick he would end up on a ventilator in the Intensive Care Unit for weeks with pneumonia. We made a simple blinking system for yes or no questions and a picture board of some common conversations items for more complex conversations.

Since he was already paralyzed from the neck down and now, he could not talk, which left him the only way to communicate was with his eyes.

When my father was already in his room laying down, we would do whatever he needed such as scratch his head, straighten out his legs that were cramping, empty his urinal or change his TV channels. Slowly, I began to learn to anticipate my father's needs or as soon as I would be out of reach, he will summon for me to come do one more thing for him.

This would frustrate my younger self, but I adapted. I would say between seven and seventeen years old my patience was being molded by these little things that seemed to irritate me. Seemingly fighting against the fact that I was the only one with a father who could not be more involved with me, I taught myself that life is not about focusing on the bad all the time.

I began to force myself to notice the positive that was around me every day. I would focus on whatever made me feel good regardless of how small or unimportant it may seem. Anything from the green grass dancing in the breeze, to a free large fry in my McDonald's bag I did not order.

I began to understand that even the negative experiences I was having were provided for a positive impact, I just had to look for it. Like when I applied for a promotion twice and wasn't accepted, or when I drop my coffee and don't have time to get a new one.

Whatever the example, it is goodness in the possibility that something positive and life changing is just around the corner. This is when I started to open myself up to the opportunities of being the beacon of love, light, and healing.

I was grateful to my father every day and extend this feeling outwards to others who may need some inspiration in their lives. I found I have much to share with whomever would say yes and hear my words.

I took my career right into the medical field when I was sixteen, just a Junior at Springfield High School. I had already been working parttime at a couple fast food places since I was fourteen but could not train or be certified in anything in the medical field until I was sixteen.

There was a school program off campus that would give students a chance to learn a trade and career in lieu of school credits. I eagerly signed up for the Health Occupations I class studying and becoming certified as a Certified Nursing Assistant (C.N.A.). As soon as I received my passing test results, I went to my local nursing home and applied to work the evening shifts after school.

They hired me and I stayed there for a couple of months before moving on to a nicer nursing home closer to home. My second year of this program was when I was seventeen and a Senior in high school.

I took the Health Occupations II class and trained to be an Emergency Medical Technician (E.M.T-Paramedic). I loved the training and hands on experience being in an ambulance answering 911 calls and being a part of the patient care in a highly stressful and fast environment.

There was a day the emergency calls would not stop long enough to allow the ambulance crew to drop me back off at the home base. I needed get to my classes, but that was so much more exhilarating than school. That was a crazy emotional day after seeing and working on so many emergencies back-to-back for about six hours. I decided I would just stay a C.N.A. at the nursing home since I was already used to working with handicapped elders who were just like my father.

Here, I worked in all kinds of different units that had special care for each one. Since my father was what is called a 'complete care' kind of patient, I was great at caring for those who needed the most help since I do that every day at home.

I even moved around within the facility working on every floor, taking care of every resident there, and worked every shift. I even worked double shifts many days a week. I stayed there for years until moving into a new career in the medical field when I knew my father was not going to be alive much longer.

I eventually entered Medical Billing in the call center, working for many more years while climbing my way up to Management. Working in a structured office setting from eight to five Monday through Friday with an hour lunch and two fifteen-minute breaks was completely opposite from working in a skilled twenty-four-hour nursing facility that offered less breaks and never closed.

When March 2020 came around the stories on the news surfaced more regarding a deadly virus spreading out of control causing extreme illnesses and deaths at an alarming rate.

At that time all my medical certifications for C.N.A., E.M.T., C.P.R. were long expired by over a decade so I could not offer any part time help to the overflowing medical facilities. My Fiancé and I were planning a wedding, honeymoon and family summer vacations since school would be out soon.

My soon to be stepson was in college and my preteen daughter was wrapping up fourth grade. We decided to slow down the planning and see what was going to happen with our jobs and the kids' schools.

Like most of the world, we thought it would only take a few weeks to pass and we would be back to normal. Well, we were all wrong!

I recall the chatter though out the office, and from those in my personal life about all the potential problems that they could be facing. Some were panicked and understandably unreasonable levels of anxiety over what to do if their jobs shut down or their childcare centers.

Others became increasingly worried and became depressed about their elders or families. Families were scattered across the world. Many had parents and grandparents in nursing homes and hospitals where visitors were no longer allowed. They were gravely worried about their parents with Alzheimer's and how they were going to handle the days and weeks ahead.

Without family coming to see them, and keeping their daily routines, how would they survive? Those kinds of patients are dependent on a strict routine and a pattern of care to keep them calm and focused on short term goals.

This helps to increase their mental and emotional positivity because being lost in their own minds is extremely scary, overwhelming, and lonely. There were mothers giving birth alone with no visitors allowed, and small children in the emergency rooms alone because only medical providers were allowed to be around the patients. All to reduce the risk of exposure to any other persons in the families.

People from all over the world were franticly trying to get back to their homes. Meanwhile, airports were shutting down one at a time and, eventually there were specific bans on all travel. A shelter in place order was handed down by the State of Illinois putting all non-essential workers on a stay-at-home lockdown and were urged not to leave their homes.

Parents with young children, behaviorally or physically challenged children, were desperate to figure out what to do as their childcare and social services was either shut down or left in limbo.

I observed those around me as many individuals were unprepared, unknowledgeable, and some decidedly unwilling to change. I was probably one of few around the world that was not worried at all. I seemed to be completely prepared for what was becoming a chaotic situation.

I had faith in our Center for Disease Control to come up with protocols, rapid testing, and quick vaccines. My lifetime of adapting to fast and stressful changes left me with no doubt I could handle this flu like virus in my household.

I had received a notification from my daughter's school that when she came home that night she was to just stay at home until further notice. A couple days later I got the notice from my work that we too were gearing up for intensive screening procedures and quarantine protocols for anyone who becomes ill or someone in their household had an array of symptoms.

Quarantine for anyone with any headaches, stuffy or runny nose, loss of taste or smell, body aches, vomiting, nauseous, earaches, or fatigue were quarantined to their homes for fourteen days. They cannot have contact with other members of the household either to prevent it from spreading and keeping six feet away while wearing masks around them.

After the fourteen days they must be cleared by a negative test and twenty-four hours symptom free before returning to their families, communities, or jobs. I know right?

Yes, that is what everyone else thought. Many considered these mitigations an attack on individual freedoms. I mean this is America, Land of the Free! I knew exactly why all these seemingly unnecessary mitigations were necessary to protect all those who had compromised immune systems, pregnant women, newborns, elderly, and not to mention all the healthy citizens too.

In less than one week my entire daily life went from being on top of the world to find that I now must rethink how I handle everything and organize my time and tasks while in this unfortunate and yet eerily familiar situation.

Schools were shut down across the county, my eleven-year-old daughter immediately transitioned to remote online schooling and was now home alone every day to finish out fourth grade.

I am an essential worker in the medical field that is still required to go to work Monday through Friday. My employer was not set up early on for mass remote work for my call center so working remote with my daughter at home was not an option at that time.

Working from the office meant I must check on my daughter and eat lunch with her before heading back to work since she would be home alone all day. My husband James was also an essential worker who works for the State of Illinois.

He was also required to report to work during the shutdown. In the afternoons he was also a part time personal trainer at a gym and had to temporarily stop working with clients and found himself with a bit of extra time. We were not so worried about the missing money since we both still had our full-time jobs.

There is a little to do list that I made up on whim when I was younger to help me get through some tough times. There is quite a lot about my childhood that most don't know about, however I became a strong independent successful woman.

My mother was an alcoholic drug addict, and when I lived with her, we moved a lot, I lost friends and belongings, was in a foster home for a while, and have woken up in different states because my mother was running from her problems.

I decided I needed a way to get through my chaotic life with a positive agenda. I came up with 'Accept. Adapt. Achieve.' First, I must accept the changes that are being presented or displayed before me. Second, I must adapt to a new structure and compromise my time management to satisfy my needs to reach my goal. Lastly, to achieve- a goal must be set.

The goal to achieve could be anything from just to make it through today, make a phone call about a bill, or get that promotion. No matter what kind of day was given to me I was just happy I had a day to be alive or be among friends and family.

Adapting was a lot harder since we live in a very fast paced, get it done, multimedia type of environment where there is less patience and generosity, compared to when my father was dealing with the Polio virus. During the COVID outbreak, we were forced to stay at home, yet during the Polio outbreak, it was a voluntary choice.

Per the New York Times Coronavirus (COVID 19) virus global tracker it has killed over 6 million people worldwide between 2020 and 2022 with vaccines and boosters made in 2021.

All of us in our little family of four were vaccinated or boosted when it came time. Unfortunately, not as many people worldwide chose to be vaccinated so we are still fighting the virus mid-2022.

I had many goals that I wanted to achieve through this awful turmoil being forced upon every single human on Earth. Since I come from a place of nurturing the sick, helping those in need, and simply not being afraid to learn new things or get my hands dirty, I needed a plan.

First, I was responsible for my daughter and myself while James was responsible for himself and his son. Then a few rules in place to ensure all participants understood their roles. Unfortunately, no more hanging out with friends in person, sports, parks, and recreational fun anymore.

All gatherings were held virtually on FaceTime, Zoom or Teams applications that allowed for groups of people to see and hear each other at once. Our hands must be washed all the time and antibacterial soap was placed in all bathrooms and kitchens.

Every car, purse, backpack, gym bag and doorway had hand sanitizer bottles in all various sizes. I personally made sure all handles, knobs and surfaces were cleaned a couple times a day and sanitized just as if my father was in the house again.

James and I would go to the store, and we planned each store we needed to visit and why. We made sure we distanced ourselves from others, wearing our masks, and getting in and out as quickly as possible to decrease amount of time in public which reduced our exposure risk.

I decided to buy a sewing machine, fabric and all the supplies needed to make homemade masks since those were becoming extremely hard to find. YouTube had some great tutorials, and after watching a couple of useful videos I found a pattern I wanted to try and ended up making about a hundred masks for a lot of people across my personal landscape.

I first made homemade masks for my immediate family and friends, then made some for the thirty employees on my team as well as some for my husband's coworkers who requested them. I did not charge or make profit from these masks and only accepted donations of fabric and supplies if they wanted to contribute in any way.

Many found themselves paralyzed with an unknown fear of 'what if,' 'when will it,' and 'why won't people just.'

What if we catch the virus, or what if we cannot purchase hand sanitizer, or the groceries we need? Then it turned into when will it stop? When will the shortage of toilet paper, masks, and cleaning supplies be over?

When will the schools and daycare open back up so we can all go to work? I was not prepared to be a full-time working mom in the daytime, and a stay-at-home mom in the evenings, but I did the best I could with what I had.

During the 2020 shutdowns, I also focused on wedding planning. I could not shop at bridal stores because they were not essential businesses. Instead, I focused on ordering decorations and party favors online for the Halloween wedding since they think it will only be a few months to get over this virus outbreak.

We spent the next few months working on ordering supplies for decorations, painting and constructing the favors and pieces of décor for the tables while in a three-month lockdown.

We even worked on our wedding invitations and mailed them out on May 4, as our way of sending them off to friends and family with good energy like the famous quote in one of our favorite movies, Star Wars' "May the force be with you."

A couple months later it was about the end of June when Illinois said we could start going out and being in crowds with no more than ten people. We were encouraged to maintain a six foot distance and wear masks to avoid possible exposure, especially if your group was indoors.

Eventually, the amount increased to fifty people, and yet still encouraged to remain distant to each other. Now we are at the point in our wedding planning where we needed to have a couple different back up plans because it is June, and we could only have fifty at the wedding and fifty at the reception at that time.

As we got closer to the October 31st wedding date, mitigations had not changed, so we decided to have just family to the wedding ceremony and split up the guests at the reception. Family would be the first half of the guests.

They could follow us from the wedding to greet us, eat some food, see the first dance and they could trick or treat at the reception and get home to really trick or treat with their families.

Then we allowed our coworkers and employees to the last two hours of the reception to eat and mingle. We did our best not to mix too many guests at a time to maintain social distancing. Potential exposure was at a minimum all while letting wedding guests to trick or treat before and at our wedding.

All in all, we planned a successful and beautiful Halloween wedding. It was sixty degrees and sunny with a slight breeze. The full moon was beautiful that night. My bridal party was dressed as witches with Mercury colored dresses, black cloaks, small and dainty witch hats.

My maid of honor was my oldest friend and my bride's maid was my newest friend, they held homemade besoms (witch brooms) while my daughter was not a flower girl, but the beholder of my light, the one who leads me down the path of happiness in my darkest times.

She wore the same black with hat and held a light lantern adorned with Plum colored flowers and dangling crystals with a glowing candle inside.

My husband and I decided we would not have our honeymoon right away since travel was still a gamble especially out of the country as we were planning to go to Iceland.

We decided to just have it a year later during the last week of October in 2021. We planned to drive to Manitou Springs, Colorado instead to visit his son who was in the

Air Force and a fireman for the next town over in Colorado Springs. We never thought it would be two years later and we would finally feel some relief from the CORONA virus.

We soon began filling our hopes for the future. I can let my daughter walk to the park and socialize with her friends and have sleep overs again. She can participate in school sports and activities again. We no longer must quarantine because we went somewhere.

Life is slowly getting back to where it was, but we all have either depression or anxiety to get through from the chaos COVID put on our hearts and minds for the last two years. Now it is time to redo my goals to Accept, Adapt, and Achieve this part of our lives after COVID.

May 23, 2022, just over 2 years since COVID rampaged through America, I was diagnosed with COVID. I was able to quarantine myself and keep my family from being exposed or catching it with my lifetime of training.

About the Author
Jennifer Lieswald Caruso.

I was born January 28, 1981, in Springfield, Illinois. My mother was a L.P.N. and my father was the Administrator of a Nursing Home. While my parents worked within these skilled nursing facilities, I found friendship and reward in helping the elderly at an early age.

By the time I was sixteen and in high school, I was a C.N.A. working in a nursing home after all day at school. The following year as a senior, I took classes to work towards becoming a Paramedic.

Later at the age of twenty-seven, I become a mother to a beautiful daughter who is now a talented and sought out artist. After working hands-on with patients for thirteen years, I changed careers and found myself in Customer Service managing the medical billing department of a clinic.

At thirty-nine I was married during the COVID pandemic on Halloween 2020. My husband is a guard for the Secretary of State and a personal trainer. He has two sons who are living on their own and making the best of both their lives.

Hereafter I will explore about finding the strength and courage to fight the demons of society, overcome obstacles, and become the best self we can while facing the worst of times. Finding the will to get up every day to move forward and help others who are struggling.

This journey through a pandemic is both exhilarating and exhausting. I will tell you the stories of how my family survived the COVID pandemic as well as how my father survived the Polio pandemic in the early nineteen fifties, spending the next sixty plus years as a quadriplegic. His legacy gave me the knowledge and strength to get my family through the pandemic we were forced to survive.

Chapter 18

Losing My Mom, Finding Myself

By Shelley Crouch

Losing the only grocery store is devastating for a small community, especially its senior citizens. But in my case, losing the grocery store led to losing my mother.

When she found out our grocer was closing soon, my mother, Julie Rea, was devastated. She would wear her mask, but she wanted to get there one last time and tell each employee how much they meant to her and how she loved the assistance they gave her.

But she never got the chance. In her distraught state, my mother, who had suffered from hypertension for twenty years, backed into her garage door as she departed for the store. As you can imagine, her blood pressure sky-rocketed from the stress. It took her a while to get the bent, heavy garage door off her car.

She grappled with the awkward door alone. Then she

realized it had left her home compromised. Because it wouldn't close, someone could enter her home through the kitchen. So, she pulled her vehicle part way into the garage and left the mangled door part way down so that no one could enter her garage and, thus, her house.

This whole time, her blood pressure was through the roof. Frantic over the store closing, she was now discouraged and embarrassed over backing into her door—another expense.

She texted me, sharing her misfortunes and inquiring about the number of our garage door guy. At dinner, I told my husband, John, I was worried about her. She had texted me earlier that day about her blood pressure.

Her cardiologist had her take it while he was on the phone with her after her recent echocardiogram hadn't given them any clues as to why it was staying so high. He said he would change her meds again. Also, I knew she was likely beating herself up about backing into the door for the fourth time in two years.

After supper, I got a call that would forever change my life. My mom called me with chest pain. I raced to her home, three blocks away, calling her nurse friend and the ambulance enroute. We waited in our masks for what seemed like an eternity for them to come.

I felt frustrated and upset because I knew I couldn't go with her, having just seen our local hospital's post on Facebook. Even people who drove their loved ones to the hospital had to wait in the parking lot. My mom's friend and I told my mom we loved her as they put her in the ambulance. She told us the same.

I did not know this would be the last time I would hear her sweet voice. Yet, I have repeatedly played this scene in my mind and heart. They ran some tests when she got to the local hospital and then transferred her to a larger hospital, hoping to save her through surgery to repair an aortic aneurysm brought on by years of high blood pressure. Mom's time in the hospital was surreal.

Because of the state and hospital's restrictions for the pandemic, I could not stay with or even visit her. Of course, many friends with loved ones in the hospital could have video chats or at least phone calls with their family, but Mom's nurses offered me no such frills. Mom took her phone with her, but was too weak to use it herself, so they locked it in a cabinet in her room.

I suppose this was because their cardiac care unit was crazy busy, and they were just a few weeks into a slew of new hospital protocols for this new highly contagious virus. But, unable to visit or talk to my mother, I was determined to find ways to encourage her.

I found out the hospital had something called Email-a-patient, a service where people could send an email through the hospital's website, and they would print them and take them to the patient's room. So, I rallied every friend and relative she had.

Later, I talked to a nurse and asked if they had been giving these printed emails to Mom, and she knew nothing about this service. How could they not know about it? It was on the website. Surely other people had used it, and the nurse had seen them come through before.

Fed up and determined to do whatever I could so my mother would not feel alone, I had the social services department check into it. Of course, no one knew where any of those emails went. But they agreed to figure it out. When they finally figured it out and sent it to me, it contained fifteen pages full of greetings to my mom. Sadly, this didn't happen in time for Mom to see them.

I'm sure the cardiac nurses and the hospital were overwhelmed. Still, I called and spoke to her nurses at least twice daily for updates on her condition. Then on Sunday morning, three days in, they intubated her and put her on a respirator without asking or talking to me.

I felt sucker-punched when the nurse told me. When I asked why, he explained that he was trying to give her oral meds that morning, and it seemed as if she would aspirate trying to swallow them.

She was so out of it. Finally, her nurse felt he had to intubate her before she choked. Then later, they inserted a feeding tube. This use of machines to keep her alive was upsetting on many levels. I found myself holding my breath several times that day, and this continued for several months.

My mom had worked as a social worker in our local hospital for years before her retirement. She served as a hospice social worker for the last several years of her working life. She had stressed over this time that she *never* wanted to be put on a respirator.

Of course, I'm sure they sedated her as soon as possible, but I could imagine her fighting them as they put that tube down her throat. She always stressed to me the importance of quality of life. She told me many times she never wanted to be kept alive by machines. Finally, the nurse told me they had to sedate her heavily because she was agitated and tried to pull at the equipment when she wasn't—my poor mom.

My mother's health declined every day after that. They kept delaying her surgery, explaining that she was not healthy enough for it. The trouble was that she needed the surgery to get better, but she needed to get better to survive the surgery. We were all just spinning our wheels.

I called our local hospital and, after several phone transfers, got to the correct department and had them send Mom's living will to this hospital. Once they received it, they scheduled a conference call with my brother and me. Then, they had me come to the hospital, and I had to go through a whole proof of wellness protocol to get to that department.

I had to fill out a health survey with many questions about any symptoms I might have experienced, and they took my temperature. The good news was that I would be allowed a short visit while I was there. At this point, I hadn't seen my mom for ten days.

When I went to the hospital to discuss Mom's care plan, I brought a photo of Mom and a short biography Mom wrote for a book she was in for them to tape to her wall. I wanted those taking care of her to see her as she was before and, hopefully, also have things to say while they took care of her.

I knew she was unconscious, but I hoped they spoke to her. In the past, I had seen on the internet a nursing home that made a small notebook about each patient. They wanted staff and visitors to know what each person had been like before they came to need round-the-clock care. It humanized the patients.

I thought that was so cool. There is a lot of research about talking to sedated or otherwise unconscious patients. I knew this because of my mom, who stressed it to the families of her hospice patients. My heart broke that I couldn't be doing this myself. At the very least, I hoped those allowed in her room spoke to her.

They mentioned later that they were so glad I brought it, and reading the bio and discovering my mom had been a hospice social worker made them want to do their best to give her the type of end-of-life care she'd given others. It was a joy to know that they read and appreciated it.

At the care meeting, we sat six feet apart in face masks in a vast room with my brother, who lived in Nevada City, California, on speakerphone in the middle of the room. They discussed the slim likelihood that Mom would survive the surgery, that she was not strong enough for it, and that she was worsening by the day.

They discussed the likelihood of the need for extended care for an extended period and possibly for the duration of her life. They also spoke of a tracheotomy and a tracheal tube. This news was very discouraging to hear.

They realized they were not following her end-of-life wishes by having put her on a ventilator and feeding tube. So, the doctors asked permission from my brother and me to take her off the ventilator. They explained it was clear from her living will that this was what she wanted. She had made this choice and had not taken it lightly. She made it with wisdom and research from years of experience in the field. Hospice care had been her specialty, and she was very familiar with living wills.

The good news was that they would finally let us see her one at a time for a total of two people for her entire stay. The bad news was that she was never conscious again from the day they put her on the vent more than a week before.

My brother flew home the next day, and the day after that, we took turns talking to her before and after they removed the vent. Unfortunately, we weren't allowed to both be in her room at the same time. We hoped perhaps she could hear us even though there was no response. While with her, I called her close friends and relatives and let them say goodbye via speakerphone held near her ear.

I was so blessed to hear these sweet goodbyes. It was a sad day, but it made me realize the significant impact my mom's life had on many people. They spoke of her love of people, her loyal friendship with them, her caring personality, and her gift of including everyone. They spoke of her wit, sense of humor, and beautiful singing voice. It was inspiring.

Mom lingered, and our time was up, so we reluctantly left to come back the next day. The nurse called me early the next morning, April 29, 2020, and said Mom's breathing and heart rate had slowed, and she didn't have much time left. Did I want to talk her out?

Over speakerphone, I told her again of our love for her. I assured her she was a great mom and Nana and that we would miss her. I told her it was okay to go. We were saying goodbye, but I knew there were so many who would greet her on the other side. The nurse then said the Lord's Prayer, and the heartbeat monitor's bleating became solid. My mom was gone.

****

Losing my mother devastated me. We were very close. I talked to her on a near-daily basis. She was my mother, friend, and one of my biggest encouragers. Going through a loss like that during a quarantine was unlike anything I'd ever experienced.

When a family member dies, other family members

travel home. Friends come by with casseroles. You have a funeral visitation with a receiving line full of people who share memories of your loved one. But the COVID quarantine had changed all of this.

Airlines had travel restrictions, and my kids all lived out of state. COVID vaccinations didn't exist yet. Traveling and gathering in groups put people at risk. My husband was still recovering from his heart attack a couple of months before and was in five comorbidity high-risk groups.

According to state guidelines, the funeral home could only have twelve people attend her service. The employees numbered about three, so I figured nine more, less than the number of her immediate family members. It honestly didn't seem worth the expense or the risk.

We decided not to have a service. We'd do it later. My brother, Steve, who came to Illinois a couple of days before Mom died, stayed a few days after. I can't imagine having gone through this loss without him, and I felt guilty for not going out to be with him when our dad died several years before. But I had been in Texas for my son's graduation from the police academy at the time.

I decided that if we couldn't have a service, at the very least, I would write a kick-ass obituary. I did my best to include a short history, funny family stories, and the like. I believe it was around 1,500 words. I was in a rush to get it out, so I couldn't edit it 500 times as I preferred, but I think it turned out well. Several people reached out to me to say they had enjoyed it.

My husband was my rock. He still took care of everything at home during his busy planting season. Yet, I longed for our kids. Mom shared life with us and meant something to each of us. Besides the everyday moments of ordinary life, we shared many pivotal moments with her—births, birthdays, holidays, graduations, and weddings.

I needed them so much, but travel seemed an unnecessary risk. We all thought this quarantine would be over soon and that we could get together then. I spoke to my kids many times on the phone.

Other friends and family called and texted as well. One sweet lady brought us a casserole. What a godsend! I pray I never forget how special that one gesture made me feel at that moment and pay it forward.

Several people sent flowers. Another thing that blessed me immensely was receiving more than a hundred sympathy cards. These were touching cards with personal notes inside. I even got a sympathy card on behalf of a *dog* in Portland, Oregon, that my mother followed and encouraged on Instagram.

My mom loved sending cards to people with thoughtful hand-written notes inside. I can't tell you how special each card was—it was like getting a hug in the mail.

Unfortunately, I've not always been the best at sending cards. I meant to but rarely did. But receiving all these cards with heartfelt notes inside spoke to me about the power of the written word, and I resolved to pay this forward as well.

One day in my grief, I realized I could state the date I last hugged each of my family members. I don't remember ever thinking about such a thing before this time. However, I often wonder if anyone else had this same thought.

We had just moved into a new home a few months

before Mom died. The new house gave me an incredible blessing that spring—an ever-changing flower bed. The previous owners of this house had planted a beautiful variety of perennials, and it seemed as if every day I went outside, a new flower greeted me.

These flowers were such a gift. I had not toiled for any of this beauty, and here it was to meet and comfort me every day. My mother loved planting flowers, so each flower and butterfly reminded me of her. When you couldn't go out into the world of people, it was beautiful to enjoy this world of wonder.

Not long after Mom's death, I made a book of her watercolor paintings. I wanted to share some of these paintings with her family and friends, but I also wanted copies of them to keep. It occurred to me that this would be a way for all of us to have them.

Unfortunately, some of the paintings I found were unsigned, so I contacted her friend and watercolor teacher, Shirley, to see if she knew if they were Mom's work. The book I created of Mom's watercolors turned out beautifully and was a lovely memento for those who wanted one.

When I talked to Shirley, I lamented that I, too, had always wanted to learn to paint. However, I felt I wasn't good at art and was too left-brained. I didn't think I could do it. She assured me this was not true.

Shirley missed my mom as I did and suggested I take lessons with her as therapy for both of us. It was risky to meet with someone, but each of us had a tiny circle of people we interacted with, and we decided it was a risk we both felt was worth taking.

I am so thankful that we did. It was great therapy for us both and gave us some outside human contact when such a thing was scarce. I told Shirley that I had often wished to make a field guide, like the Peterson Field Guides I enjoyed, but for children. My granddaughter was a toddler, so I thought to make a board book field guide on flora and fauna of our pond.

The first thing I attempted to paint was bluegill. I painted my first painting and discovered a new passion. I have created four board book field guides for toddlers as of this date. I have also had my watercolor paintings at two art galleries in four different art shows.

What a world these lessons opened for me. Now that I'm vaccinated, I meet weekly with a small group of ladies in the back room of a nearby art gallery to visit and work on our latest projects together. What a joy it is to create both art and new friendships.

Had it not been for the quarantine, I would not have felt I had time to learn to paint. Even though our lives are mostly back to normal, I make time to paint. It has become vital because it is therapeutic for me, and I enjoy it. Every time I paint, I feel close to my mom, as if she is still here.

One of the most painful things that happened to me after Mom's death occurred because of many things that happened simultaneously. We were all still primarily trapped in our homes, and social media was our main lifeline to each other.

While my political views have changed over the years, and I don't currently align fully with either party, my mom has always been a Democrat. I live in a small conservative town, and many of my mother's friends and my friends are Republicans. As I was home alone grieving the loss of my mother, my Facebook newsfeed was filled with posts hatefully bashing all Democrats and, thus, my dead mother.

These would have been hard to take anyway but coming at the hands of people I considered dear friends of myself, *and* my mother made them more painful. That they arrived via folks who call themselves Christians was incredibly ironic, given the hateful tone they carried.

Each post I read felt like they were throwing stones at my mom. Now mind you, not all my friends behaved this way. But enough that it devastated me.

One day, someone I considered a dear friend, who had also told me how much she loved my mother, shared a revolting post towards all Democrats, calling them a host of hurtful insults. I just broke down. Alone and shocked, I began to sob. But it wasn't just this awful post; I was grieving how people now treat each other in our polarized social media world.

I couldn't contain my grief for my mom any longer. I sobbed so hard that my body shook. Yet, no one was home to comfort me. I felt like I couldn't breathe. There was a sharp pain in my chest.

I considered going to the hospital but didn't. John was still busy in the field, and I didn't want to cause him extra stress. I was sure I just needed to calm down, breathe deep, drink water, and relax, and I would be fine. I read later that broken heart syndrome causes chest pain and sometimes damage to the heart. Who knows?

Day after day, I saw this online behavior continue— posting, sharing, and liking hateful posts towards whole groups of people I loved by other people I loved. Finally, crushed and shocked by the lack of empathy and understanding for one another, I withdrew.

It was a dark time for me and left me changed. When you insult the beliefs of an entire group of people, it makes them feel disrespected, unseen, and unheard. I see this behavior displayed by friends on both sides. I felt it more deeply than ever before because I was vulnerable.

Both sides could learn that such behavior will never influence their neighbors as they wish and may unintentionally harm loved ones. Although, as far as I can tell, they don't seem to care.

I did notice one pastor in town encouraged members of his church to respond in love and prayer and not lash out with political statements—what an excellent example of love. Not surprisingly, he also held a panel to discuss racial issues during the racial unrest of June 2020. Again, I was very impressed with his actions.

Eventually, I unfollowed everyone but close family on Facebook, not even following all my family members depending on their online behavior. I needed to protect my mental health. I would have gotten off entirely if I had not been a social media manager for over a dozen Facebook pages.

Others must've shared my experience because Facebook added the "care" emoji in April 2020. Over time, I slowly followed people who behaved lovingly, regardless of politics. I learned that for my mental and physical health, I needed to remain distanced from toxic behavior and be kind to myself by surrounding myself with kind people.

When someone dies, many tasks remain for those who survive them. For example, our mother left my brother and me with a car, a house, furniture, and personal possessions.

In normal times, taking care of all of this is a monumental task. However, at the beginning of a national lockdown, it seemed daunting.

I needed to take care of the forty-four house plants my mom left behind. I had already taken care of them since she went into the hospital, but I don't have my mom's green thumb, and I didn't want them to die, mainly because they were so important to her.

They had already gone three weeks without her speaking to them. My mom fully believed that talking to plants helped them grow.

I took four plants for myself and texted photos of the rest to my kids and my mom's friends. Then I gave away the rest to whoever would take them. Sadly, I didn't know until it was too late that my mother babysat four plants for a friend wintering in Texas. I accidentally gave away her friend's plants to someone who took them out of state; one was even in a handmade pot. I felt terrible when I realized what had happened, but there wasn't anything I could do.

Before I could sell Mom's home, I needed to go through and give away or sell all her belongings. And let's just say that Mom liked to collect lots of things. One lady posted on Facebook that Mom was a "save a broken piece of pottery because it holds memories" kind of lady.

Initially, I needed to find and take care of all the bills and paperwork, some of which I would need to keep paying until the home sold, and some I could cancel. Mom had so many papers that it was hard to know what was essential and what was not.

Some of these tasks were easier for me because when the national quarantine shut down most things, all our calendars were suddenly open. However, some of these tasks were more difficult, as many government offices were closed.

Sometimes I found things that made me laugh. For example, while looking for essential papers, I found an alphabetical accordion file of various documents, some important, some not. On the front, my mother had written a key: B-Banking, C-Correspondence. But here is the funny one: H-Humor, see L for Laughter.

Sure enough, filed in the L section, I found scores of comic strips cut out of the newspaper. I took a video and showed my kids. *Oh, Mom, you were a treasure.* From time to time, I slip these comics into cards I send out, laughing as I do.

Next was the daunting task of going through all her belongings. Typically, you would have an auction out in the yard, but our state had stopped public events like these because of the quarantine. I eventually found an online auction service.

While going through her belongings, I found many treasures. One was a cassette recording of several radio shows Mom had been on in the early 90s. As the DJ, Jason Flick, of WEIU Radio, interviewed her, he asked her questions about her life, and it was so cool to hear the stories she told. And she sang several songs. It was beautiful.

I found other recordings of her singing too, and I made a YouTube channel called Julie Rea, Folk Singer, and I put all the recordings there so that any of her friends or family can listen to them whenever they want.

Another thing I discovered was reel-to-reel tapes my dad and mom sent to each other when he was on a hardship tour for the Air Force in the Aleutian Islands during the

Vietnam War.

It was a joy to listen to their voices and feel the love in their early marriage, as they had divorced when I was twelve. And what a pleasure to hear myself as a toddler playing in the background.

In September 2020, my mom's monthly Sunday brunch group wanted to have a small, private, socially distanced outdoor memorial service for Mom. What a blessing this was to me. They were planning it. I only needed to show up. This service would finally give me some closure. And a chance to share my grief with others.

It was a beautiful day, and they had decorated an area in the pines with chairs spaced twelve feet apart, flowers, and beautiful quilts. I wore one of my mother's shirts and her jewelry. A group of ladies played music; different ones shared stories about Mom. We played a recording of Mom singing and sang along with her.

A few of us shared brief masked hugs with our breath held—a strange thing I would notice and be part of many times during the quarantine. Physical touch, especially hugging, is necessary to so many of us.

Yet, hugging felt like a risk in an unknown world of a highly contagious disease that could be deadly to some and would not even cause a symptom to others. But it remained a significant part of human interaction that we all craved.

I brought a box full of my mom's treasured rocks and seashells from her home and let the ladies pick out whatever they wanted, and the rest we placed among the pines.

I brought a small container of some of Mom's ashes, and during one song, those who wished to take part took some ashes and sprinkled them in Mom's favorite area of the pine grove. It was all lovely and moving. Finally, we retreated to the front lawn, where we could sit outdoors and socially distanced for conversation and refreshments.

My mom is gone, and I still miss her like crazy. I'm sure I always will. But I believe she lives on in me. I'm thankful for how I've learned to keep her memory alive. I am grateful to be writing more and creating art. Both are excellent therapy.

I will try to honor my mom with how I live my life and show love to those around me, treating them with love and respect regardless of their different belief systems so that I can be a part of making this world a kinder and more loving place, as my mom did.

Like her, I want to stop and listen to people and hear them without judgment, looking for what we have in common instead of where we disagree. I want to honor her memory with how I treat others.

About the Author
Shelley Crouch

Shelley Crouch hails from Casey, Illinois, home of 3,000 people and a dozen World's Largest things, two of which she can see from her living room window.

Living in the home of the Big Things in a Small Town, Shelley has big dreams in a small town.

Besides being a writer/author, she also fancies herself an artist/illustrator. She has written and illustrated four nonfiction board books for toddlers: *Pond Life, 2020, My Bug Book, 2020, Texas Wildlife, 2020, and My Bird Book, 2021,* filled with simple watercolors and text.

She is working with Crystal Heart Imprints Publishing to make these available in a more economical paperback form. Until then, you can check them out through the interlibrary loan program of the Illinois Heartland Library System.

Shelley was recently part of Past-Forward's Memoir Writer's collaborative memoir collection, *For the Record*, published by CHI in November 2021.

She is currently working on a collection of her, and her late mother's memoirs tentatively titled, *Like Mother, Like Daughter: Memories Across the Generations.*

And to keep things interesting, she is crossing over to fiction. She is working on a mystery for middle-grade children titled, *Only the Dog Knows,* illustrated with simple pen and ink drawings, and an illustrated storybook for preschoolers, *Emily's Moon,* with prints from acrylic paintings. She plans to publish all these works in 2023-2025.

Shelley has been married for thirty-eight years to John Crouch. He is the most encouraging and supportive husband, and she is most grateful for that. He is a sixth-generation farmer and guitar-playing singer-songwriter with two CDs out. They have three talented children and two delightful grandchildren.

So thankful to have found CHI Publishing, Shelley enjoys the incredible support they provide to their writers throughout the process.

ABOUT CRYSTAL HEART IMPRINTS (CHI)

Crystal Heart Imprints is an independent eclectic press administered by a collective group of writers. Formed in 2012, to help inspire those who need a little push to get started onto the journey of writing.

Our motto is 'Everyone has a story.' Our hope is to encourage those stories to be written and published. Every author, or want to be author, dreams of holding that book in their hands, and we at CHI dream of making that come true.

www.crystalheartimprits.com
https://www.facebook.com/Crystalheartimprints